OLD TIME HOCKEY
Memories & Musings of a Lifetime on Ice

By

Glen Sonmor with Ross Bernstein

To Ron Peltier
The most
successful
Golden Gopher
I know
all the best
Your friend
Glen Sonmor

OLD TIME HOCKEY
Memories & Musings of a Lifetime on Ice
By
Glen Sonmor with Ross Bernstein

Published by Bernstein Books, L.L.C.
www.bernsteinbooks.com

ISBN: 0-9787809-1-4

Distributed by Adventure Publications
Cambridge, MN (800) 678-7006

Printed by Printing Enterprises, New Brighton, MN • (651) 636-9336

Photos:
Glen Sonmor: 10,14-18,20-23,26,28-30,33-34,41,52,74-78, 80,83-84, 86,89-90,95,117,122,127,129-33
Brooks family: 100,103
University of Minnesota: 26,38,42-48,102,108-12,117-19,121, 124
Donald Clark Collection: 24,36,79,81-82,87,92-94,98, 105,108,123
Bruce Kluckhohn: 114-116
Birmingham Bulls: 69-70
Mike Lamey: 50,54-63,65-66
New York Rangers: 31-32
USA Hockey: 101
Minnesota Moose: 106-107
Terrence Fogarty: 120

A portion of the proceeds from the sale of this book will benefit the Glen Sonmor University of Minnesota Scholarship Foundation. Thank you for your support!

Table of Contents

Introduction
by Ross Bernstein

To say that Glen Sonmor is a throwback would be such an understatement. He is "old-school" down to the bone, and that is what makes him one of the most colorful and popular figures in Minnesota hockey history. Whether he was punching someone's lights out as a player, or teaching the fundamentals of the game as a very successful coach, Glen has been a part of the fabric of Minnesota sports for more than half a century. This is his incredible story.

I first met Glen back in 1992 when I was in the midst of writing my first book. I had tried out unsuccessfully with the Gopher hockey team back in the late '80s and wound up instead becoming the team mascot, "Goldy the Gopher." It was a blast. Upon graduating, I decided to take all of my graduate school money and use it to write a book which would ultimately be called "Gopher Hockey by the Hockey Gopher." Against the better wishes of my parents, I then set out on a journey to chronicle the history of Gopher hockey from a large, furry rodent's perspective. Along the way, I wound up interviewing hundreds of current and former Gopher players and coaches. Early on in my adventure I called up Glen and asked if I could buy him breakfast. As a former Gopher coach he had been familiar with my shtick over the years at old Mariucci Arena and was excited to finally meet the man behind the mask.

I remember meeting him at the Thunderbird hotel in Bloomington, which, fittingly, was right in front of the Met Center — home of the Minnesota North Stars. By this point in Glen's life he was scouting with the Philadelphia Flyers, having left the Stars a couple of years earlier when Norm Green showed up and started stinking up the joint. Anyway, Glen and I hit it off from the get-go. I sat there with my little tape recorder eating a bagel and just listened in awe to this guy who just wreaked of hockey history. I will never forget how badly my sides hurt from laughing so much at all the stories he told me about John Mariucci, his hero. For me, a 21-year-old kid from Fairmont, it was a thrill of a lifetime. I mean here was a guy who actually played for an "Original Six" team way back in the day, hanging out with me like we were pals.

Glen and I would stay in touch over the years and I was able to get together with him again a few years later when I wrote a coffee table book about the history of hockey in Minnesota. We again met at the Thunderbird and I listened in awe to him tell me stories about his days with the old Minneapolis Millers, the New York Rangers, the Gophers, the Fighting Saints and of course the North Stars. I later invited Glen to the book launch party that I had thrown over at Tommy Reid's bar down on West Seventh Street in St. Paul. I didn't think he would bother coming all the way over there, but sure enough he came and what a night it was for me and my old college buddies to listen to him tell stories all night.

As a player he talked about what it was like to play with John Mariucci and later with the New York Rangers at old Madison Square Garden. As a coach he reminisced about the legendary 1981 North Stars vs. Boston "Curse of the Garden" game that set an NHL record for penalty minutes, and he told us about the time he took 16 stitches in the melon following an on-ice melee with the Detroit Red Wings. He opened the vault and let us in. It was, in a word, fantastic.

I remember looking at them all as they hung on his every word. It was magical, to see Glen hold court in front of a swarm of fresh faces who had never heard any of his stories before. And the thing that was so cool about it was the fact that Glen was just being Glen. He probably would have loved to talk to anybody about that stuff, but he made them all feel so special. Glen is the exact opposite of the Randy Moss' and Terrell Owens' of the world, he represents everything that is good about sports. He treated them with such respect and was genuinely appreciative of their glowing admiration. Believe it or not, my old fraternity brothers still remember that night like it was yesterday.

We later connected again for another book project I did about Minnesota's greatest coaches. It was there where I truly learned what a great hockey mind he was. Sure, he had great stories about beating the hell out of people, but there was a whole other side to the man that I was fascinated to learn about. Our paths crossed yet again in 2003 when Herbie Brooks was tragically killed in a car accident on his way home from a golf tournament. I had actually been working with Herbie at the time on writing a series of motivational/self-help books. When I heard the news I, like so many hockey fans, was absolutely devastated. So, I decided to honor my friend and mentor by turning our book project into a memorial to honor his legacy. Glen was one of the first guys I called to write one of the forewords for "Remembering Herbie." The other guy was Louie Nanne, who was kind enough to do the same for Glen in this book.

From there, Glen and I would see each other often at Wild games, Gopher games, the high school tourney, at celebrity golf outings and galas, and even at the annual Old Timers hockey luncheon at Mancini's over on West Seventh. We eventually got to talking and figured that we should collaborate on our own book project, which is exactly what we did. I was thrilled when he asked me to do it because I look up to him so much. He is like my grandfather and my buddy all wrapped up into one. He is such a great guy and I feel so proud to be able to honor him in this way.

The project took more than a year to complete, but it was well worth the wait. Whenever I talked to anybody about the book the first thing that I saw was a smile on their face. That is what Glen Sonmor does, he brings smiles to peoples faces. Usually, the next thing that would come out of their mouths would be a question or comment regarding how many great stories I had collected, both by Glen, as well as about Glen. To hear a Glen Sonmor story nowadays is like hearing a tall tale about Paul Bunyan — they are almost like folklore. By now I have heard them all, tweaked and embellished over the years, but they are all classic — just like Glen.

Among my personal favorites are the ones about the adventures of Glen's glass eye. He lost his real one during a hockey game in Pittsburgh back in 1955. Let me tell you, that eye has truly gotten around. It has wound up in a few drinks over the years of some unsuspecting ladies, and it even got flushed down the toilet one time too. There was the time he lost it on the bench during the singing of the National Anthem at a North Stars game, and another time when it fell out and rolled all the way down the aisle of the team bus on the way home from Wisconsin. One time Glen was in the stall of a men's room at an airport somewhere when his eye popped out and rolled into the stall next to him. So, he politely asked the guy next to him if he could please roll it back over to him. Glen said the poor bastard was so freaked once he saw that eyeball staring up at him that he jumped up and high tailed it out of there without even pulling his pants up. The best one though came after a bad call during a Fighting Saints game one time when Glen popped his eye out and offered it to the ref, telling him "Here, you take it, you obviously need it more than I do!"

Hopefully you will get to know the real Glen Sonmor in the pages of this book, both the hockey caricature as well as the person. His story is an amazing one that embraces guardian angels while centering around two driving forces, hockey and alcoholism. As you will soon learn, one of those guardian angels, John Mariucci, got him into school and into coaching, while the other, Louie Nanne, had the courage to help him defeat the stranglehold of alcoholism that had gripped his life for decades. His is a story that is both heartbreaking as well as inspirational. From it, however, you will learn about determination and perseverance. His honesty and candor when it comes to fighting the demons of alcohol might even make you stop and reflect upon your own life.

Glen comes from very humble and modest beginnings up north of the border. His father was an alcoholic who wasn't around very much, so his mother showed him the way. They didn't have much money either, but she always made sure that Glen was able to participate in sports. It would become his salvation, his savior. It didn't matter what season it was, Glen would be outside playing something or another, having fun while escaping some of the cruel realities of life. He dreamed of one day playing in the National Hockey League and it was a dream that would ultimately come true. The journey to get there, as well as the journey that robbed him of that dream are what this story is all about though.

When I was going through all of Glen's clippings and photos from the past 75 years, I remember coming across an article from August of 1960 by noted Hamilton Spectator writer Gary Lautens. It was a retrospective piece about one of the writer's childhood heroes, who, at the time had played in the NHL and was on his way to coaching greatness. In it, Lautens described his hero, Glen, as the "Hamilton schoolboy who might have been the most blessed athletically of them all." He referred to him as a "bony kid who could play hockey, baseball, football, basketball, or snooker, with the poise expected only in a pro... and an excellent student too." He even referred to Glen's boyhood home as a "landmark" which might someday be an historic attraction among the likes of George Washington, Joe DiMaggio or Syl Apps.

Glen played all sorts of sports, but it was hockey that would become his passion. As a player, Glen was tough as hell and protected his teammates out on the ice, no matter what. As a coach, Glen was no different, always standing up for his boys, regardless of the consequence. Glen was best in the heat of the battle. He wasn't a great tactical X's & O's type of a guy, but he could always get his players fired up and ready to take on the world. He had the ability to take players of lesser ability and give them roles that would somehow inspire them to play way beyond their limits. Glen also loved tough guys who could stir up the pot and beat the crap out of a few people every now and then. He is a throwback, a one-of-a-kind, the epitome of a players' coach.

These days, in addition to serving as a scout for the Wild, Glen does color analysis on the radio for his beloved Gophers. At 78 years young he is still a whirling dervish of energy, and is still having a ball. As a radio commentator you are supposed to be an objective journalist, but Glen said to hell with that right out of the gates. In fact, his unabashed devotion to the Gophers comes out loud and clear in his broadcasts. Case in point. Back in 2005, when Phil Kessel scored the game-winning goal that beat rival Wisconsin, Glen shouted out "Take that you stinking Badgers!" Glen is a proud homer and makes no apologies for that whatsoever. Then, as a scout for the Wild, Glen works the local college and high school beat. His knowledge of the game is still second to none and as the other scouts will tell you, "he sees more out of that one eye than most of the other guys do with two."

While both jobs keep him busy, they also afford him the opportunity to remain firmly entrenched into his two passions: hockey and recovery. Glen gets up every day and heads over to the nearby Thunderbird Hotel, where he orders two poached eggs, bacon and coffee for breakfast. Then, after reading the hockey box scores from the night before in the paper, he meets with other recovering alcoholics from his fellowship. Some days they just shoot the breeze and tell stories. Others, however, might mean talking somebody down off the proverbial ledge. Either way, Glen is there for them. He has been sober for 25 years now, an accomplishment that he is more proud of than anything in his life. It defines who he is and where he has come from. At the end of the day he unwinds by watching some TV, preferably a hockey game.

And then, when he is just about to hit the sack, he thanks God for another day without alcohol. For Glen Sonmor, it truly is one day at a time.

I recently went to a Wild game with him and got to hang with him all night. What a treat. Walking through the concourses of the Xcel Center with Glen is probably a lot like walking into Cheers with Norm Peterson. It was a constant parade of "Gleeennnns!" as fans and onlookers paid their respects to a real life hockey legend. Some just wanted to shake his hand and tell him a quick North Stars story, while others whispered proudly to him that they too were "friends of Bill W.", which is a reference to the fellowship that Glen belongs to which saved his life. He greets them all with the same smile and enthusiasm.

You know, when I was trying to come up with a title for the book I immediately thought about a classic line from one of my all-time favorite movies, "Slapshot." It goes: "Old time hockey, coach, like Eddie Shore, Dit Clapper, Toe Blake ...". It is a line I hear often while playing in my old man senior league games even to this day. The line is repeated a couple of times by the legendary "Hanson Brothers," the lovable goons who stole nearly every scene in the movie away from the Oscar winning star of the film, Paul Newman. "Old Time Hockey" is so fitting because Glen actually discovered the real life Carlson brothers at a try-out when he was coaching the WHA's Fighting Saints. He fell in love with them because they were tough as hell Iron Rangers who loved to play physical and mix it up out on the ice. He signed them and then assigned them to the team's minor league affiliate in Johnstown, PA.

It was there, as members of the fictitious Charlestown Chiefs, where they would gain infamy as the Hanson Brothers. In reality, the Hansons are Jeff and Steve Carlson, along with Dave Hanson. The third brother, Jack, got called up by the Saints when it came time to start shooting the film, so Dave filled in. So when you think about it, Glen really is one of the last living links between the old school and the new school. Case in point, while most kids today would never have a clue as to who in the hell Eddie Shore was, in reality, Glen actually coached under Eddie for a year back in the 1950s up in Springfield, Mass. And don't worry, there are plenty of hilarious stories in the book about he and old "Blood and Guts" Shore too.

As I sat back and reflected upon completing the book, I couldn't help but come to the conclusion that this book, among other things, is also a love story. That's right. And I am not talking about Glen and either of his two ex-wives, I am talking about Glen and his sincere love for his best friend and mentor, John Mariucci, the "Godfather of Minnesota Hockey." The two first met back in 1949 as teammates with the minor league Minneapolis Millers. Glen was just a tough kid on his way up the ladder, while John was a grizzled old veteran at that point in life, on his way back down from serving as the resident enforcer of the Chicago Blackhawks. The two hit it off immediately and became inseparable. When John saw Glen he must have thought he was looking into a mirror, only 15 years earlier. It would be the beginning of an amazing saga that will weave its way throughout the book, culminating at the end with some classic stories. Trust me, it will be worth the wait to get to that chapter.

With the tragic passings of John Mariucci in 1987 and of Herbie Brooks in 2003, it is safe to say that Glen is now "Minnesota's official hockey ambassador." Others would say that if John was the godfather of Minnesota hockey, then Glen would certainly have to be the grandfather. Either way, his legacy is far reaching. That was so important to me in tackling a project like this too, to celebrate not only Glen's achievements, but his legacy as one of the game's true patriarchs. Sure, he has won some honors and accolades along the way, including being awarded the NHL's prestigious Lester Patrick Trophy; the Hobey Baker "Legends of Hockey" award, not to mention his recent inductions into the University of Minnesota and Manitoba Halls of Fames. Aside from all of that, Glen's legacy will be about giving back to the game he truly loves.

Now, we must issue a caveat of sorts at this point. You see, at 78 years young, Glen's memory isn't perfect and he wants the readers to know that he tried his best to remember things as best as he could. So, please forgive him if he gets something wrong, and please forgive me if I didn't catch it. I am also proud to announce that a portion of the proceeds from the sale of the book are going to benefit the newly created Glen Sonmor Scholarship Fund at the University of Minnesota. Glen's pal Louie Nanne spearheaded the project and I couldn't be more thrilled to help such a fantastic cause. I hope others will be inspired by Glen's story and contribute to it as well.

Well, there you have it. I hope you enjoy reading about one of the game's great iconic characters. It was a real honor and privilege to be able to celebrate one of the hockey world's greatest treasures. Glen's colorful personality has touched so many lives over the years in ways he will never know. He has truly made a difference in the world, especially to me. My life is so much richer now that I have gotten to know him as closely as I have. Beneath that gruff exterior is so much wisdom. I am so proud to be able to call him my friend. It is amazing for me to think about how far my life has come since that day back in 1992 at the Thunderbird, when I got to meet this guy for the first time and listen to his stories. It is pretty neat to think that I was able to make a career out of that little rodent memoir, and that I am now working on my 40th book. So, it's only fitting that I come full circle back to the guy who helped me start it all, my buddy Glen — Mr. Old Time Hockey.

Oh, and one last thing, when you are reading the book and listening to Glen speak in your head, you might want to hear the words in a thick Canadian accent. Really emphasize the words "out" and "about" and "against," I think it will make the entire experience much more authentic and way more enjoyable... Eh? Cheers!

Foreword by Lou Nanne

I first met Glen back in 1967 at the University of Minnesota when I was coaching the freshman hockey team under John Mariucci. When Mariucci left to join the expansion North Stars that year, Glen was brought in to be the new head coach. I stayed on and worked with him for the year and really enjoyed getting to know him. What a guy. We hit it off together and quickly became friends. I could see his passion for the game and just how knowledgeable he was about hockey. Glen was an excellent teacher and the players really respected him. I learned a great deal from him in that short amount of time, both on and off the ice.

We stayed in touch over the years while I was playing with the North Stars and he was coaching the Gophers. Later, in 1978, when I took over as the North Stars' General Manager, one of my first jobs was to hire a new head coach. I told the ownership group that my first and only choice was Glen. They then proceeded to tell me that there was no way that was going to happen. Glen had coached the WHA's St. Paul Fighting Saints, which competed directly with the North Stars and nearly put them out of business a few years earlier, and they couldn't support that decision. So, I told them that they had better find somebody else to run their team because that was who I wanted to hire. They then asked me to wait outside while they discussed it. Five minutes later they came out and gave me the green light to go ahead and hire him, which is exactly what I did. It was one of the smartest decisions I ever made because just a few years later he wound up leading the team to the Stanley Cup Finals.

I originally put him in charge of player personnel to help facilitate the merger with the Cleveland Barons that off-season. Glen is and al-

My old buddy Louie

ways has been a wonderful judge of talent. He sees things out on the ice that other people just can't see. As a coach, he was just top notch. In fact, I would say hands down that he was the best coach that the North Stars have ever had. He was extremely passionate about our organization and just poured his heart and soul into everything he did. The team always came first with him and he was absolutely committed to winning . I put a lot of faith and confidence in Glen's opinions about hockey over the years. Whether he was coaching or scouting or working with player personnel, he was somebody who I really trusted and somebody whose viewpoints I truly valued.

As a coach, one would categorize him as a demanding individual. He expected 100% effort from his players and he held them accountable. Most importantly though, his players believed in him. He gave them strength. He gave them backbone. They knew that he was there with them, no matter what. If the gloves came off, they knew that Glen wanted to be out there in the middle of it all. He would implore all of our players to be on the outside of the checks, rather than on the inside — where they were getting hit. His leadership style gave them confidence and emboldened them.

He worked hard with the players so that they were properly prepared both physically and mentally each game. His players were in top condition. He was adamant when it came to fundamentals as well. For instance, during practice he insisted that the players always stayed onsides. He worked on that during their scrimmages and made them aware of it at all times. As a result, we hardly went off-sides come game time. He also put guys out there in situations that favored their strengths. He was a very good judge of talent and knew what situations were the best for each player. He wanted them to do their jobs, and if they didn't or wouldn't, then he wanted to get somebody in there who could.

He was always coming to me to try to convince me to acquire this guy or trade that guy. He loved the good guys, but hated working with players who weren't as committed as he expected them to be. I used to tell him 'Glen, my wife can coach Neal Broten, Craig Hartsburg and Bobby Smith for God sakes — you earn your money coaching the most challenging guys in our line-up. I remember during the Stanley Cup Finals against New York back in 1981 when I sat down with him before the opening game out in Long Island to talk about the line-up that night. I pulled out a piece of paper with 13 names on it and asked him sarcastically if any of the names on that list looked familiar to him. He says, 'What do you mean? Sure I am familiar with them, they are all playing tonight.' I then looked over at him and said 'That's funny, because over the course of this season you wanted me to trade all 13 of them at one point or another...'. We both had a good laugh over that one.

I would also say that Glen Sonmor the player was very different form Glen Sonmor the person. As a player, Glen was extremely competitive. He was very physical and wasn't ever afraid to drop the gloves. His teammates loved to play with him. Beneath that gruff exterior, however, is a kind, giving, caring, wonderful human being. He has gone through a lot of adversity and challenging times in his life though, which I think has only made him stronger.

As many people may know, Glen battled alcoholism throughout his career but thankfully was able to beat it. He has been sober for 25 years now and I couldn't be prouder of him. I was right there with him during some of his darkest days and saw how destructive this disease can be. When he was coaching the North Stars and was going through some really trying times we made efforts to get him cured. We had a couple of interventions with him and he would battle it and fail. It was so hard to watch and to see how badly he wanted to beat it. I felt very strongly about him as a person and wasn't going to abandon him. I just hoped that Glen was eventually going to beat it. I didn't ever want to give up on him and thankfully he was able to overcome it. We put a lot of pressure on him to get clean and we had to hold him accountable. We had to get firm with him and we did because we wanted him to get his life in order before it completely collapsed around him.

I remember when he was coaching the Stars and we were playing up in Montreal. He had fallen off the wagon at the time and was trying to avoid me. He would do little tricks to lay low, like holding up a newspaper so that you couldn't see his eyes, or he would even wear a lot of cologne in order to mask any scent of alcohol on him. Well, I sat next to him on the team bus that next morning after he had been drinking and I was really disgusted with him. So, I leaned over to him and I said 'Glen, I know what I am going to get you for Christmas this year.' He looked over at me and said 'Yeah, what's that?' I said 'A new glass eye.' 'Why is that?' he said very curiously. I said 'Well, this one will be all bloodshot, so it will match your real one. That way you won't look so weird when you try to fool me after you've been out hitting the sauce.' I didn't hear a peep out of him for the rest of the day after that.

When I finally had to let him go as the North Stars coach, it really hurt. He had promised us that he was going to stay clean and sober, and when he fell off the wagon we had to do what we felt was best for him. So, we helped him by sending him to a treatment center, where he was able to sort some things out. That next year, when he came back, we tried like hell to make sure he was going to stay on track. I remember even putting a clause in his contract that basically said that we could fire him with no recourse if he started drinking again. The doctor who ran the intervention program advised me to do it. What Glen never knew though is that I was never going to actually follow through with it if push ever came to shove. I just wanted it there as an incentive for him. Glen really wanted to beat it and we all knew that. So, if he did fall back, then we all knew that we were just going to have to work harder in order to help him.

I remember the night back in 1983 when he finally hit rock bottom. It was after a game in Pittsburgh and he had gotten into some trouble. I was in Vancouver at the time and flew back to meet with him as soon as I heard what had happened. He came into my office and the first thing he said to me was 'Louie, I need help.' That was the first time in the 17 years that I had known him that he said he needed help to beat his illness. That was it for him, something clicked. We got him some help and from that point on he has been clean and sober. It is hard to believe that was a quarter century ago.

What is so amazing about Glen though, is the fact that during the entire time since he has been sober he has been out there helping others who also suffer from the disease. He is such a generous, selfless person and has really made a difference in a lot of lives over the years. He has been just an unbelievable asset to countless people who have had similar problems. He cares for them, he listens to them and he is there for them. He does whatever he can to help them, whether that is talking to them or meeting with them at all hours of the night. He just sees it as his duty and I really admire him for that. I don't know of any individual who works harder at trying to help others. What an amazing guy.

It is so great to see Glen as happy as he is and doing what he loves. As a radio analyst with the Gophers, he is one of the very best in the business. He is so enjoyable to listen to and really has a passion for what he is doing. Then, as a scout, Glen is a fantastic judge of ability and character. I talked to Doug Risebrough when the Wild were about to hire him as a scout. I said that Glen works very hard and gives terrific assessments of players and most importantly, he is right with these young kids much more than he is wrong. He just has an uncanny ability to see the little things in people and can really tell if they are going to make it at this level or not. That is a unique skill that is very valuable to an organization and Glen has more of it than most people I know in the business.

As for his personal life, Glen lives very modestly and doesn't really care a whole lot about material possessions. Glen's castle is a hockey rink, not his house. He is more at home there than he is anywhere else, and that is usually where he would rather be. Hockey truly is his life. As for Glen's legacy in the world of hockey, it will be different things to different people. First and foremost, however, is his love and respect for the game. He will always be remembered as a competitive player, a great coach, manager, scout and announcer. He has just done it all at all levels of the game.

To me, his legacy will be that of a passionate, loving, loyal, caring, knowledgeable and dedicated hockey man. The bottom line with Glen is that he just loves hockey and loves to be around the game. It doesn't matter if he is watching a Wild game or a mites game, he has the same passion and interest in it. As for his legacy outside of hockey, he is just a terrific person and a true friend. He is so generous and is such a selfless person. He is also very loyal and is always there for you if you need him. You can count on him, no matter what. If I had to pick one guy to go to war with, it would be Glen, no question about it.

The two people who have had the greatest impact in my life when it comes to hockey are John Mariucci and Glen Sonmor. So, I guess when it's all said and done I would put it this way: John was like my second father, and I would have to say that Glen was like my brother. I just love the guy, how could someone not?

Ch. 1 Ohhh Canada...

My name is Glen Robert Sonmor and I was born the son of Cyrus and Kathleen Sonmor in the town of Moose Jaw, Saskatchewan on April 22, 1929. I had an older brother, Jake, and a younger sister, Kay. We lived in Moose Jaw, which was about 40 miles outside of the capital, Regina, until I was four years old and then we moved to Toronto. This was the onset of the Great Depression and everyone was moving from out west to the east, where the jobs were more plentiful at the time. It was a tough time for my family. My dad was, sadly, someone whose life was troubled by alcohol. He was a government inspector by trade, but was also a pool shark and a gambler too. He was in and out of my life for most of my childhood.

In Toronto, we lived right by this big park called Christie Pitts, which had lots of ball fields and plenty of games to get involved in. I think that this had a great deal to do with my passion for sports. I was over there all the time, playing with my friends and just being around all of the activities. I played a lot and I watched a lot, and that was where it all began for me. It was wonderful, it really was. Sports would prove to be my savior and keep me out of trouble. We would wind up moving again a few years later to another part of town, to a much bigger home which was actually a boarding house that we were able to rent out rooms from. I remember a few of my uncles living up above on one floor, as did this beautiful blonde woman who used to date Turk Broda, the famed Toronto Maple Leafs goalie. It was certainly an eclectic mix of people who we had living in there, that was for sure.

By now athletics had become the absolute focus and driving factor for me in my life. In the summertime I would go to Elizabeth's Playground, or "Lizzy's" as the kids used to call it, all the time to play games with my friends. There was a guy there who was absolutely famous in Canada by the name of Bob Abate, who served as the playground director there. He was also a legendary youth sports coach and somebody who all the kids really looked up to. He coached literally hundreds of championship teams in basketball and baseball over the years and was a real role model for a lot of kids up there. He was for sure my mentor, I thought the world of that guy. In fact I would say that he had the biggest influence on my athletic career of probably anyone. I just wanted to be around him as much as I could and

My big brother Jake and I

would even help him out just so I could stay at the park longer. He would send me out to get his lunch for him and he would get a sandwich for me too. Then, I would hang out there all day long, playing whatever intramural activity was going on. He even kept statistics for us about our progress, or batting averages and about our team standings. We just couldn't wait to get up in the morning and run down there to do it all over again. It was fabulous.

As for hockey, I first began skating on a big rink that the University of Toronto would flood every winter on the school's football field in Varsity Stadium. My mom would buy me a season pass for $4 bucks as an early Christmas present and I would spend every waking moment over there playing with my buddies after school and on the weekends. There were no teams for us or anything, it was just pick-up hockey. They had different rinks set up for the various ages of kids, so that made it nice too, to be able to play with your friends without having to worry about the bigger kids pushing you around out there.

As a kid I looked up to the Toronto Maple Leafs. Of course there was no television back in the 1940s, so I would read the newspapers and listen to them on the radio in order to follow them as best as I could. I used to follow guys like Teeter Kennedy, Turk Broda and Red Horner. I also looked up to Rocket Richard, who played with the Montreal Canadiens; and Gordie Howe, who starred for Detroit. Those guys weren't that much older than I was, but I enjoyed following them. They were just fantastic players.

Well, we lived in Toronto until I was in the sixth grade. From there, we moved just over the border to a small town called Ridgeway, right outside of Buffalo, NY. It was during WWII and times were tough. My dad got a job in a war manufacturing plant there and we wound up staying for one year before moving back to Hamilton, which was back just outside of Toronto. It was at about this time when I had my first memories of my dad's alcoholism becoming a problem. I remember one incident in particular where he really let us down. We were all set to move out of our rental house in Ridgeway for the move back to Toronto. My mom, along with my brother and sister and I, got all packed up and were waiting for my dad to show up with the truck so that we could load it up and hit the road. We had to be out of the house that evening in order for another family to move in. So, we packed up our belongings and waited outside on the curb for him to show up. We waited and waited. Meanwhile, the other family had moved in

My mother and father

15

and were bringing us out food and water. We just sat out there on our furniture until he finally showed up at around four in the morning. Sure enough, he had been out drinking and gambling, which really made us all pretty upset. I would later learn in my own recovery from alcoholism that people who suffer from this disease are not very reliable or dependable. It was sad, but we made the best of it.

I started the eighth grade in Hamilton and wound up moving into what was called a "war-time" house, which was located across from the Hoover plant. It was on 872 Barton Street, I will never forget it. It was at this time that I also started to play organized sports on actual teams. While I had always played youth sports up until that point, I had never really been on any serious teams. I remember my basketball team winning the Hamilton City Championship that first year, we had a really good team and that was a lot of fun. I also played on my first organized hockey team that year as well, which was very exciting for me. I will never forget getting my first ever hockey jersey with my team logo on it, it was so special. I was lucky too in that my house was right across the street from a huge sports complex that included the Hamilton Tiger Cats football stadium, a baseball stadium for a minor league team of the St. Louis Cardinals, a huge indoor swimming pool, and a great big open field called Scott Park — which was grassy in the summer and icy in the winter. They would flood it when it got cold and it made for a whole bunch of hockey rinks. So, I got plenty of ice time whenever I wanted it.

My youth hockey team was really good. In fact, four of us would go on to play professional hockey, including myself and Steve Kraftcheck, who both played in the NHL. It was a different era back then. Our parents never really came to our games or practices. We just played for the love of the game. Hockey was not a part of the schools back then either. It was run by the local police departments, which organized leagues in order to help keep kids off the streets.

Well, after grade eight I had to decide which high school I was going to go to. There was Delta Collegiate, which was tougher and more academically based, or Central Tech, which was a technical trade school. Most of my friends were going to Tech because it was easier, but I wound up going to Delta. I chose it for two reasons. First, I was a good student; and secondly, I was just awful at anything mechanical. I remember my

1946-1947 "AEROVOX" JR. B. - O.H.A. SEMI-FINALISTS
Back Row, L. to R., N. Baikie, J. Anderson, G. Steeves, S. Kraftcheck, "Pinky" Lewis, B. Maxwell, F. Bergeron, J. Norris, A. Aitken, M. Shewfelt, E. Shewfelt, D. Eisthen. Front Row, E. Busch, D. McKay, P. Soutar, J. Strong, D. Leeson, J. Loader, J. Taylor, A. Garbas. MISSING: G. Sonmor, T. Russell.

My 1946-47 Aerovox Junior B team, we played at Mahoney Park...

buddies building coat racks, book ends and bird houses, and I couldn't build a thing. I will never forget my shop teacher at junior high school, this little Scottish guy, who used to get so mad at me whenever I would try to build something and mess it up. One day he was really impatient with me and he said in his thick Scottish accent "I shall throw you out the window, I shall, and the window shant be open!". So, it was the right choice to go to Delta, and fortunately it worked out very well for me. It was a great school and I had a lot of opportunities both athletically as well as academically.

Playing high school sports was wonderful. I played football and basketball on the Delta sponsored teams, and also played baseball in the summertime with an independent league. The school didn't even bother to offer baseball back then because they figured the cold weather wouldn't allow for a full season anyway. As for hockey, I played at the midget and juvenile levels in the various leagues that were available at the time with all of the other kids while I was in high school. It was very unorganized. My first midget team was called "Mahoney Park," and we played against other neighborhood teams from around Hamilton.

Believe it or not, my best sport at this time was basketball. My Delta basketball team won a couple of city championships back in the early '50s and we were really good. The school really got behind us and we were the big men on campus. Playing both sports was tough though. I would play basketball after school and then go to hockey practice at night. Somebody would have to drive me over to hockey practice after I got showered up from basketball and it certainly made for some long nights and weekends, that was for sure. Eventually, something had to give.

My basketball coach was somebody who was very, very important in my life. His name was George Ferris and he was just a great guy. Well, when I was 16 he came to me and told me that he was not going to let me play both basketball and hockey that next year. He saw how hard I was pushing myself and thought that I was going to kill myself if I tried to keep up that crazy pace. I was really upset about it. I mean I had led our basketball team in scoring that year and didn't want to give it up. I will never forget what he told me to convince me that hockey was the right sport for me. He said "Glen, there aren't any basketball scouts coming up here

THE NEW CHAMPS — Delta Collegiate's senior basketball squad, conquerors of Westdale's Dawn Patrol in the city high school title series just concluded. From left to right, back row, D. H. McWhirter, physical director; John Maycock, guard; Murray Heuchan, guard; Les Bridgehouse, guard; Jack Mattys, forward; Jack Knight, forward; George Ferris, coach. Front row, left to right, Bob Heal, forward; Glen Sonmore, forward; Gordon Marsh, forward; D. Stevenson (captain), forward; Bill Ferrier, centre; Sam McBride, centre.

My Delta High School basketball team

looking for five-foot-ten shooting guards. There are plenty of hockey scouts though, and that is where you should focus your efforts." He was right, but I just loved being the hero in school and getting all of that attention. I mean in hockey we were playing in these old, dark run-down arenas at all hours of the night with nobody there to root us on. So, I told him that I was going to choose basketball and quit the hockey team. He couldn't believe it.

I played basketball that entire season and then as soon as we were done, I was able to join a junior B hockey team, the Hamilton Lloyds, which were run by a pretty famous coach in Hamilton at the time by the name of Pinky Lewis. He was an African American coach who I really looked up to, just a great guy. Anyway, one of my buddies, Andy Garbas, had gotten scouted to play baseball down in South Carolina, and that opened up a spot on the team. Once he left, I took his spot. Now, the junior ranks were for the older kids and they played a lot of games. Fortunately for me, our team went on to play in the Ontario championship game that year and I was able to get plenty of ice time despite joining the team so late in the season. As luck would have it, because our team had made it all the way to the Finals that year, I got noticed by a bunch of scouts for a new Junior A team that was just starting out in the nearby town of Guelph. They had been out scouting the top Junior B teams in the area and asked me if I wanted to join their squad, the Biltmores, that next season. I was so excited.

I was in grade 13 at that point, which is unique to Canadian schools, and Junior A hockey was the top of the line for amateur players in Canada. The Biltmores were a farm team of the NHL's New York Rangers and I knew that if I could play well with them then I might have a chance to play professionally down the road. The coach of the team was Bobby Bauer, who was one third of Boston's famous "Kraut Line" along with Milt Schmidt and Woody Dumart. He had just retired from playing in the NHL and I was anxious to learn as much as I could from him. He even allowed me to continue to play football that next Fall. He liked kids who were good athletes and had a well-rounded background in all sports. I was so grateful, because I

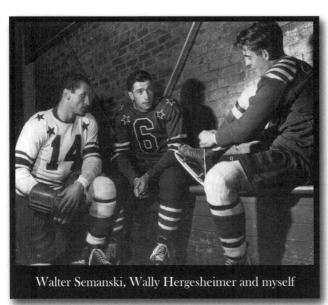
Walter Semanski, Wally Hergesheimer and myself

loved football and didn't want to just give it up.

You know, as I look back and think about that I can't help but wonder about kids today and about how they are becoming so specialized in just hockey. I feel very strongly that they too should be given every opportunity to play other sports and to have fun. Sure, when they get older they can focus on just one sport, but for the most part kids who are good all-around athletes go on to become good all-around students and citizens. I look at kids like Paul Martin, who starred for the Gophers before going on to play with the New Jersey Devils. He was a tremendous high school football player and even set some state records as a wide receiver. He was an outstanding student in the class room too, which is so important. He was able to do both and still excel. So I would advise parents and coaches everywhere to look hard at that and try to encourage the same for their kids.

Anyway, I was fortunate to be able to play football with all my buddies and still play hockey at a very high level during my last year of high school. It was tough, but I made it work. I would go to school at Delta on Mondays and then head up to Guelph, about a half an hour away, for a few days to play hockey. I would come back to Delta on Thursday to go to school and practice football, and then we would have our football games on Friday nights. It was fun but it was also controversial too. Some of the kids protested me doing both sports and I even got investigated by the school board. They were figuring that I was just going to quit school immediately following the football season. Well, luckily the superintendent, a guy by the name of Dr. Price, allowed me to play. He was a big hockey fan and made sure I was able to do both sports. I excelled out on the ice, averaging about a point a game as a left winger. I remember getting paid $25 per week to play for the Biltmores, $16 of which went towards room and board at a boarding house. It was like a giant frat house, that place, the entire team lived there. Those were some wild times, let me tell you.

I eventually graduated with distinction from high school, which was something I was very proud of. At about that time I went to my basketball coach, George Ferris, for some advice. You see, because my father was in and out of my life as a kid, I tended to gravitate towards my coaches for guidance. So, I asked him what he felt I should do with my life. I needed some hard career advice and I knew he would give it to me straight. He said "Step one: ask yourself what you like to do and what truly brings you joy. Step two: determine the profession that is most closely aligned to that and start to research it. Step three: go and get the best possible preparation for that career that you can, preferably by going to college. Step four: don't worry about money and success right away because if you love what you really want to do and have a passion for it, then you will eventually be able to make a good living at it." "Most importantly," he told me, "you will be happy in your life and won't have to work at a job where you will be staring at the clock all day wishing you were somewhere else."

I knew that I wanted to be a teacher and a coach, and that was all the advice I needed to reassure myself that I was making the right decision. I loved sports and wanted to continue in hockey for as long as I could. I also knew that I could start my schooling right away and start both careers at the same time. That was the best advice I ever got. You know, that was 62 years ago and I remember it like it was yesterday. I tell people that story all the time whenever they ask me for career advice or if they are struggling with addiction. It just makes so much sense to me.

My big plan from there was to go on to college, probably at the University of Toronto, to play either football, basketball, baseball or hockey, and get a physical education major. You see, I had also been playing some semipro baseball during the Summers as well, which was a lot of fun. I knew at that point that I wanted to teach and coach, so that was what I set out to do. Ultimately, however, I wound up signing what was known back then as a "C-form." You see, in those days there was no professional draft for hockey players. Professional teams would sign up kids via that form, which basically said that if you ever played professionally, then they owned your rights. They would then pay you like $100 bucks upon signing it, followed by $100 each year that they wanted to keep you around in the junior ranks until you signed with a minor league team.

Meanwhile, my former Junior-B coach, Pinky Lewis, had become a scout for the minor league Cleveland Barons — an American League franchise that had close ties with the NHL's New York Rangers. He worked it out so that I was able to sign with them, which was ultimately the beginning of my professional hockey career. I will never forget taking that first $100 bucks and running down to meet my mom to show it to her. She was shopping at the time and I told her that she could buy anything in the store, my treat. I thought I was rich.

From there, Cleveland invited me to attend their training camp in

Here I am with the Wheat Kings

Brandon, Manitoba. I went and wound up making the team, the Brandon Wheat Kings, a top-level junior team that was a developmental team for kids on their way up the ladder. I remember scoring four goals in one of our first games against the Winnipeg Monarchs, while also taking care of their tough guy in a pretty good fight. At that point, I could tell that I was ready to play at that level and was prepared to put off my schooling for a bit while I pursued my hockey career. I knew that it would be there for me down the road, so I just decided to enjoy the ride and see how far it would take me. My focus then became that of making a living in hockey, which really drove me. I obviously didn't come from any money, so I was determined to be able to take care of myself. I also set a goal for myself to one day play in the National Hockey League. That, I thought, would be a dream come true.

Our Wheat Kings team went on to dominate the Manitoba League and then won the Canadian junior championship that year. I lived with a billet family there, really nice people. It was much nicer living with a family than it was living with a bunch of filthy hockey players, like I had done in Guelph. The players on the team, many of whom would go on to become very successful in business and in life, were very bright people who were education oriented and that gave us a really good team chemistry. I will never forget all of my teammates and I singing "I'm looking over a four-leafed clover" on the bus rides home from our games. Those were great times. Overall, it was just a good year to work on my hockey skills and to get plenty of ice time.

My nickname at the time was "Scrawny Sonny," because I was so small. I worked out and got bigger though and could take care of myself out there, which was really appealing to the Cleveland organization. I worked hard, went from 150 pounds to 175 pounds, and gained a whole lot of confidence. I finished second in the league scoring race and was ready to take the next step, which just so happened to be with Cleveland's top minor league team, the Minneapolis Millers.

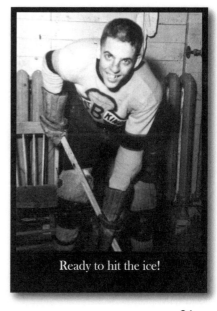

Ready to hit the ice!

Ch. 2 On to the Land of 10,000 Lakes...

By now it was 1949 and I was excited as hell to move south of the border. The Minneapolis Millers played in the United States Hockey League with St. Paul, Omaha, Louisville, Tulsa and Kansas City. The USHL was two rungs below the NHL, but featured some really good hockey players. We played downtown in an old rink on the corner of 28th and Dupont and were coached by Bill Cook, a legendary winger with the New York Rangers. I played on a great line with Wally Hergesheimer and Frank King. We were pretty good, in fact all of us would eventually play in the NHL.

I wound up living with one of my teammates from Brandon, Frank King, who had gotten called up to Minneapolis with me. Frank was a pretty responsible guy. He had a wife and kid back home and didn't waste any time getting situated in the Twin Cities. He rented a two bedroom place and then sub-let one of the rooms to me. It was great. I didn't know how to make toast for goodness sakes and it turned out that his wife was a fantastic cook. Now, the thing that was so funny about Frank was the fact that he was so unbelievably cheap. We got paid $3,500 bucks in salary that year, plus a $500 bonus for winning the championship, and Frank would literally not spend a dime for anything. He used his perdiem to buy all of his meals and wouldn't even buy a newspaper, figuring that somebody would set one down when they were done with it sooner or later. I will never forget at the end of the season when we were packing up to say good bye, he had 22 crisp $100 bills in his hand that he had

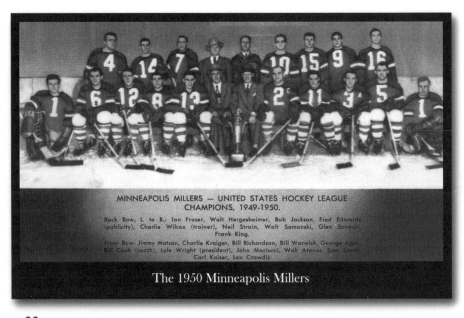

MINNEAPOLIS MILLERS — UNITED STATES HOCKEY LEAGUE
CHAMPIONS, 1949-1950.

Back Row, L. to R.: Ian Fraser, Walt Hergesheimer, Bob Jackson, Fred Edwards (publicity), Charlie Wilcox (trainer), Neil Strain, Walt Samanski, Glen Sonmor, Frank King.
Front Row: Jimmy Matson, Charlie Kraiger, Bill Richardson, Bill Warwick, George Agar, Bill Cook (coach), Lyle Wright (president), John Mariucci, Walt Atanas, Sam Lovitt, Carl Kaiser, Lou Crowdis.

The 1950 Minneapolis Millers

saved. I don't know how the hell he got by on what he did with a wife and baby, but he somehow managed. Well, Frankie went on to become a multi-millionaire later in life as a successful businessman, so he must have known what he was doing.

You see, back then there were only six teams in the NHL and all of the young players had to rise up through the minor league ranks in order to make it to the top level. The teams were a mix of really young kids like myself, who were climbing the ladder up towards the top, and older veterans who were hanging on as they were on their way down. It was an interesting mix for sure, but I certainly learned a lot from playing with some of the former NHLers out there. In fact, there was one guy on my team who would take me under his wing and truly change my life. His name was John Mariucci. He was our captain and our leader. Everybody just loved the guy and really looked up to him. We would sit in awe of him on our bus or train trips to away games and listen to him tell stories. He was so funny and could tell stories until all hours of the night. He was the only American on the team too, and as a former college graduate he loved to rib us and tease us about how dumb he thought we all were. It was all in good fun. We would all go to Swede's Bar together after games, where big John was like our personal bouncer.

John had been the enforcer for the Chicago Blackhawks for the past several years and had just played the previous season with St. Louis in the American Hockey League. He was in his mid-30s at this point but still loved to play the game. He was from Eveleth and had starred on the University of Minnesota's hockey and football teams about a decade earlier. He wanted to come home to finish his career before getting into coaching. I had heard about Mariucci as a kid. So, to get to play with him and learn the ropes from a guy like that was something pretty special. We hit it off right away, I was just in awe of him. He really taught me a lot about life both on and off the ice. He was a really respected player because he stood up for his teammates, no matter what. Like so many Iron Rangers, he was just tough as hell. In fact, when he was playing with Chicago, he was one of the most feared fighters in the entire league.

Later in my career, when I was playing in New York, I got to know the Bentley brothers, Doug and Max, who played for years with John in Chicago. They used to tell me stories about John all the time. You see, those two, along with Bill Mosienko, made up the famous "Pony Line." They got that nickname because they were all about five-foot-seven and 150 pounds, but faster than hell. The rea-

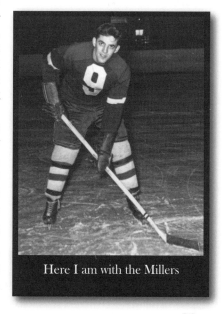

Here I am with the Millers

23

son they were so good was because Mariucci protected them like their mother. John knew his role and he loved it. He knew that he wasn't there to score 50 goals, he was there to protect his teammates. If anybody messed with those guys they were going to have to face big John.

The Bentley brothers said that playing with John made hockey fun for them again. Before John got there, other players used to intimidate them and make runs at them because they were the stars of the team. Well, when John got there it took just one trip around the league for every team to learn not to even look funny at the Bentleys. Anybody who tried anything with those guys knew that John was coming to get them. And back then you didn't have any of the penalties or rules about coming off the bench like we have today. I remember Max saying, "Anybody who tried to intimidate us had to have some pretty big balls because as soon as they went after us they would have to turn around and get ready for big John, who would come flying off the bench in a hurry. And there wasn't any doubt as to why he was coming either because he left his stick and gloves back on the bench!"

John used to love beating the crap out of guys and he was pretty darn good at it. The Bentleys told me that there was only one guy who dared mess with them, Detroit's Black Jack Stewart. They said that Black Jack would get bored out there sometimes and decide to make it interesting, so he would take a shot at one of the them just so John would come after him. Those two used to love brawling with each other. In fact, they still own the record for the longest fight in NHL history, an epic brawl back in 1946 that lasted for nearly 20 minutes. God, the crowds used to love the Detroit-Chicago games because they knew they were in for a treat. Even the referees would just sit back and watch those two go at it. And I mean it was a fight, not a bunch of grabbing and holding on to each other. In those days guys fought toe to toe, as soon as they

Here's John as the captain of the Chicago Blackhawks going toe to toe with Detroit's Black Jack Stewart in the NHL's longest ever fight at nearly 20 minutes...

grabbed on to each others jerseys then that was when the referees would break it up. So, they would just land haymakers on each other until they could barely stand up. It was great. That was when hockey was fun. Then, after the game, they would go out and drink beers together. It was crazy, but that was the kind of guy John was. He would knock you down and then pick you back up.

The funniest story I can remember about the Bentley brothers actually had to do with their dad. He was a very modest farmer from Canada who didn't have a lot of money, but was sure appreciative of John protecting his two sons. So, the first year that John was there, he told him that if he protected his sons that he'd give him a nice bonus at the end of the season. Well, at the end of the year John had kept his end of the bargain and was excited to see his bonus. Mr. Bentley then thanked him and cordially presented John with a big old cow. John, in amazement, said "That's great, but for all the punches I took for these two guys, I could've used $500 bucks or something...". God only knows what ever happened to that poor cow after that.

So, I learned the value of toughness from John and how important it was to stand up for not only yourself, but also for your teammates. That is what the hockey code of honor is all about. That was John's legacy, he protected his teammates from being taken advantage of and intimidated. He earned a lot of respect for being so selfless, that was for sure. I will never forget walking through downtown Chicago with him one time and we saw two cabbies walking towards us. The one turned to the other and said, "Hey that's John Mariucci, he fights for the Hawks...". Yes sir, he was one hell of a bruiser, and they loved him. When he lived in Chicago he would even run around with Al Capone and his mobster friends. He would tell us all sorts of crazy stories, we listened to him like little kids at bedtime. He was amazing.

Anyway, playing with the Millers was a lot of fun. We wound up winning the 1949-50 USHL championship with a record of 33-28-9. We beat the St. Paul Saints in the first round of the playoffs and then beat Omaha for the title. I will never forget that best of five series with Omaha, it was so tough. Game One was on the road in Nebraska, on this huge rink. Omaha, the Detroit Red Wings farm team, wanted fast skaters in their minor league system. So they made this enormous rink which was even bigger than an Olympic sized ice sheet for them to skate on. They were tough at home on that ice too and hadn't lost there in like 20 games. Well, our coach came into the dressing room just before the game and asked us what he thought our game plan should be for that night. Figuring we might concede that game, he left it up to John Mariucci to come up with a game plan.

Big John just smiled and said "OK fellas, all we need to do is win one game here in Omaha on this big rink in order to win the best-of-five series. We have owned them back up in Minneapolis on our tiny ice sheet and I am sure we can beat them in Games Three and Four. So, let's just throw this game and concede it right now. But, lets beat the hell out of them from the opening whistle to soften them up for Game Two. It'll be fun. I don't care if we take 50 penalties, just run those guys any chance you get out there. I will be there to protect you if things get ugly."

I tell you what, that is exactly what we did. We lost the game, 7-1, but we absolutely beat the crap out of those guys. We were so happy back in the locker room, it was hilarious. I have never been in a happier locker room with a bunch of guys who just lost a playoff game by six goals. But, sure enough, we came back and beat them badly the next night to earn a series split. Then, back on our home ice in Minneapolis, we just killed them and went on to win the championship. I will never forget John getting into a ton of fights with Omaha's tough guy, Pete Durham. John was just pummeling him, it was brutal. Yet, this kid just kept coming back for more — and John would keep giving it to him.

Well, eventually John's knuckles were getting all torn up and he could hardly hold on to his stick. So, midway through the series he skated over to Omaha's bench and had a few words with their coach, former Red Wings star Mud Bruneteau. Mud's younger brother Eddie played on their team and was a real shy kid, not a fighter by any means. John says to old Mud "Keep that damn goon Durham away from me or the next time he comes after me I am going to skate right by him and beat the hell out of your brother instead." Needless to say, that was the last time Durham skated anywhere near John for the rest of the series.

When it was all said and done I finished the season with 60 points in 55 games. I was looking forward to doing even better that next season but realized that wasn't going to happen when it was announced that the team had been sold and was moving to Denver. Shortly thereafter, myself, along with two of my teammates, Wally Hergesheimer and Sam Lavitt, got called up to the Cleveland Barons of the American Hockey

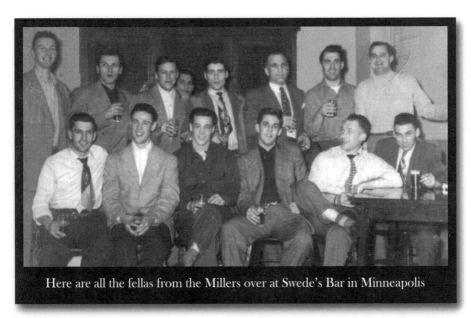

Here are all the fellas from the Millers over at Swede's Bar in Minneapolis

League. I was sad to say good bye to my friend, John Mariucci, but our paths would soon cross again.

For me, one of the best parts of living in Minneapolis was the fact that I was able to take some college courses at the University of Minnesota, where John had helped me to get enrolled that Spring quarter. John literally took me by the scruff of my neck and walked me over to the admissions office. He went and talked to Professor Lou Keller, and talked him into letting me enroll in his class late in the term. I will always be grateful to him for that. He told me that in all of his years of playing professional hockey that I was the first Canadian teammate he had known who had

Big John with the Gophers

graduated from high school. He told me that I was going to get my college degree, or else.

John would turn out to be my guardian angel, he really would. I didn't want to disappoint him so I would make the effort to come back to campus every summer while I was playing professionally to get that degree. It turned out to be such a blessing. It was tough sometimes to have to stay home and study while my teammates were out having beers at Swede's Bar, but getting my degree was so important to me. In fact, it was something that would consume me over the ensuing years.

After the season I took a few months off to go back to Canada to see my family. I then returned to Minneapolis to take classes for the second Summer session. Luckily for me, the University had accepted my grade 13 scores from Canada and counted it as my freshman year of college. So, technically I was a sophomore. I got a room in a dormitory and took as many classes as I could. It was a great time, I just loved it. I became friends with some great student-athletes who were pursuing degrees in physical education too — guys like Paul Giel, Ed Kalafat and Larry Ross, who were all legendary Gopher athletes in baseball/football, basketball and hockey, respectively. We used to get together over at Manning's Bar on Como Avenue. Those were great times.

John also played defensive end for legendary coach Bernie Bierman

Ch. 3 Ecstacy and Agony in Cleveland...

Moving to Cleveland was so exciting. I was anxious to step up my game and see how well I could do at the next level of competition. Bun Cook, the Hall of Fame winger with the New York Rangers, coached the Barons and was a real gentleman. Now, Cleveland wasn't actually New York's top farm club, but rather they were an independent AHL team that had a lot of close ties with the Rangers. So, a lot of our top players would wind up getting signed by the Rangers. Certainly that was everybody's goal there too, to make it up the next rung in the ladder — to the NHL.

In Cleveland I first lived in a hotel across the street from the arena. Later, I wound up getting a pad with a bunch of my teammates in the downtown area. It was a lot of fun being there and it was nice to be able to have a few bucks in my pocket to go out once in a while too. As a player I was coming along. I had a reputation for being a tough kid who would skate hard and not back down from anybody. I could fight and I would fight if I had to. I was pretty tough, believe it or not. I think people would have described my playing style as physical, abrasive and determined. I was an average skater, didn't have a great shot, but was able to make plays through hard work and a feisty attitude. I didn't go out looking for trouble, but if anybody took liberties with my buddy, Wally Hergesheimer, then I was going to be there to take care of him. I learned just how important that was from John Mariucci. I didn't want to be an enforcer though. That was not my role. Hell, I wasn't big enough to do that job anyway. Don't get me wrong, I wanted to score goals like everybody else. I just figured I would do whatever it took to help my team win, whatever that entailed. Short on talent but long on desire, that was me.

We wound up winning the league championship my first year in Cleveland, beating Pittsburgh in the finals. I played well, scoring 49 points in 65 regular season games, and then added seven more points in the playoffs — which was big. Following the season the team's general manager, Jim Hendy, a real good guy who helped me a great deal in my career, pulled me aside. He told me that he was going to loan me to the AHL's St. Louis Flyers that next season, 1951-

Here I am with the Barons

52, in order for me to get more ice time. He figured I would have a better chance to develop there, rather than in Cleveland, which had a lot of veterans on the team that year. So, I went there and had a pretty good season, scoring 54 points in 67 games.

I returned to Cleveland for the 1952-53 season, where I not only tallied 51 points in 64 games, but I also put up 62 penalty minutes — which the organization really appreciated. That gritty, agitating style of play would eventually get me my big break midway through the next season when the Rangers acquired me in a trade for Andy Bathgate. Well, Bathgate, who was only 19 at the time, would turn out to be a future Hall of Famer. In reality, the Rangers wanted him to get some more ice time in the AHL and we basically swapped spots. They even threw in $10,000 in the deal as well. So, when it was announced in the papers it read that I was traded from Cleveland to New York in exchange for this future Hall of Famer, plus $10 grand. I always got a kick out of that.

Anyway, I was really proud of the fact that I had finally made it to the pinnacle of professional hockey. Heck, with just six NHL teams, there were only 18 jobs for left wingers and I had one of them. What a thrill it was to play at Madison Square Garden. Then, I will never forget stepping onto the ice at the Maple Leaf Gardens in Toronto proudly wearing my NHL sweater. As a young boy growing up just outside of Toronto I had fallen asleep at night on countless occasions dreaming of that very moment. I only played in the last 15 games of the season with the Rangers, but I did manage to score a couple of goals — both of them being game-winners.

Another significant event happened in my life that Summer when I got married to my old high school sweetheart, Margaret Mitchell. You know, I really never dated too much back in high school. I was so into sports and into my schooling, that I didn't have much time for it. I did wind up dating Margaret, however, and we wound up going to the prom together. Believe it or not, we stuck together on and off from then on and

1954-55 CLEVELAND BARONS

Front (L-R): Edward J. Coen, publicity director; Emile (The Cat) Francis; Eric Pogue; Fred (Bun) Cook, Coach; Jack Gordon, Captain; James C. Hendy, General Manager; Fred Glover, Roy McMeekin, Lex Cook, Chief Scout. Seated on floor: Elmo Baumann, Stick Boy. Second: Billy Ford, John McLellan, Ian Cushenan, Gus Karrys, Joe Lund, Ott Heller, Tom Williams, Fred Shero. Third: Charles Homenuk, Trainer; Eddy Reigle, Jimmy Farelli, Steve Kraftcheck, Glen Sonmor, Eddie Olson, Cal Stearns, Floyd Perras, Promotion Director. Larry Smith collection.

eventually got married about six years later while I was in Cleveland. It was tough while I was traveling so much, but we made the best of it. She would come visit me in Minneapolis and then in Cleveland whenever she could, and I would get home to see her in Hamilton too. We didn't talk on the phone too much in those days, but we wrote a lot of letters to each other to stay in touch. She eventually went on to attend Western University in Ontario, where she got her teaching degree. Finally, in the Summer of 1953, when we were both 24 years old, we got married. She moved to Cleveland and we got a little place to live there in a neighborhood near where a lot of the other players lived. It was nothing fancy but it was nice.

The next year I started the season with the Rangers and played 13 games with them. I was there specifically to play alongside by old buddy, Wally Hergesheimer. Wally was a budding star and he lobbied hard to get me up there with him to watch out for him. That was how it worked in those days. Eventually I got sent back to Cleveland, however, when Wally hurt his leg. With him out of the line-up, that didn't bode well for my playing career with the Rangers. So, back in Cleveland I resumed my role as one of the team's top-line wingers and figured I would just pay my dues until I got another opportunity to rejoin the team.

Everything was going along fine at that point. By February I had scored 32 points in 36 games with the Barons and we were in good position to make a run in the playoffs. Then, on February 19, 1955, one of the happiest events of my life took place when my beautiful daughter Katherine was born. I remember going to the hospital and just being so excited to finally be a father. I got cigars for all my teammates, they were all so excited for me. It was just a marvelous experience.

Then, just four days later, my life was changed forever during a game in Pittsburgh. I had just scored a goal and was feeling great. Then, midway through the game, I was standing in front of the net trying like hell to screen the Hornets goalie. I was jockeying for position as my defenseman wound up on a slap shot from the point. That defenseman was Steve Kraftcheck, my old childhood buddy and next door neighbor from Hamilton. I knew that he had a hard shot and I knew that if I was in position, that I would be able to either tip it in or maybe get a rebound goal.

Just then, Steve

My wife and newborn daughter

wound up and let one rip. As I turned to see where the puck was, I felt the impact of the puck hitting me square in the left eye. It had gotten deflected and ricocheted right into my face, I didn't even see it coming. It hurt really bad and I knew I was in trouble right away. I wasn't knocked unconscious, so I could hear all of the players screaming for the trainer to hurry out there. There was blood everywhere. I remember my trainer telling me it was going to be OK because the puck had hit me above my eye. Then I heard one of my teammates tell me it was going to be OK because the puck had hit me below the eye. I knew that at that point I was probably going to lose my eye. I couldn't see anything out of it and it was pretty bad. I just remember my teammates all coming over to me as I was being helped off the ice, telling me it was going to be all right. I remember thinking to myself, what if this is the last time I ever play hockey again? Sadly, it was.

I immediately went to Mercy Hospital in Pittsburgh, where the doctors started to look me over. I was really scared. I was just 25 years old at the time and I had my whole life ahead of me. I just had a baby a few days earlier and didn't know what I was going to do. Here I was in a hospital in Pittsburgh not knowing what my next move in life was going to be, and there my wife was in a hospital in Cleveland with a newborn baby. It was a tough time, let me tell you. I had a great doctor though, Dr. Rohm, who took really good care of me. He explained to me that I needed to keep immobilized in order to have any chance of recovering. So, I wound up staying in that hospital for about six weeks, which was really difficult. I just wanted to get out of there in the worst way. I remember my wife finally coming to visit me after a week or so. We just hugged each other and cried. It was the happiest and saddest I had ever been. We just tried to stay positive and look forward. That was all we could do.

One of the first phone calls I got in the hospital was from my old friend John Mariucci. I will never forget laying in bed and hearing his gruff voice on the other end of the line say to me, "Hey kid," he used to always call me kid, "don't you worry about a thing. I have arranged for you to come to Minnesota where you can finish your degree and be my freshman coach for the Gophers." I couldn't believe my ears. Wow, it was like God himself had spoken to me. It was like an awakening, it really was. It was at that point that I realized that John was my guardian angel, and that he was watching over me.

A lot of different players would come visit me in the hospital

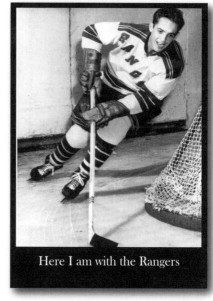

Here I am with the Rangers

and that meant a lot to me. The Barons even had a benefit game for me a few weeks later against Pittsburgh, where all of the proceeds from the game went to my wife and I. They later presented us with a check for about $10,000 bucks, which was a whole lot of money in those days. We would use it to buy our first house. It was a really nice gesture by the organization and we really appreciated it. The team went on to make the playoffs that year and I was really rooting for them. I followed them closely and that gave me something to do.

Knowing that I had a job waiting for me gave me a whole new sense of purpose in life. I was thrilled to be going back to Minnesota. I had been going there during the Summers to take classes and I would now finally have a chance to finish my degree. Despite all of the drama in my life at that moment, I was really excited about the idea of being back with John at a place that I just adored. Plus, I was going to be working on a team that had just gone to the 1954 NCAA Finals, which was exciting too. I had followed them and was heartbroken when I found out that they had lost to RPI in an overtime thriller in the championship game. What an upset that was. I mean Minnesota had four of the six All-Americans in college hockey that year in John Mayasich, Dick Dougherty, Ken Yackel and Jim Mattson. I knew that it must have been so disappointing for John to have lost that game because he so desperately wanted to win it all and prove that Minnesota kids had what it took to be the best in the country.

Years later, Dick Meredith, who was also on that team, told me that after the game John was so upset that he actually cried. He said that all of the players huddled around him to shield him from the press and their cameras. I couldn't even imagine seeing John shed a tear, he was the toughest man I had ever known in my life. He must have really been hurting inside. Anyway, knowing that I had that to look forward to gave me hope, which was exactly what I needed at that difficult time in my life.

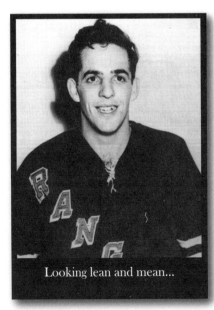

Looking lean and mean...

Eventually, after six weeks in the hospital, Dr. Rohm told me that they were going to have to remove the eye. They had been hoping for the best, but realized that my situation was not going to improve. I was ready to accept that and move on. So, they went ahead with the surgery and I got fitted with a glass eye. From there we wound up moving back to Hamilton, where I just relaxed and took it easy for a while. We both had a lot of family there and it was nice to have some time together with our new daughter.

Later that Summer we then packed up and made the move to Minneapolis. We wound up getting a little place in St. Paul at the Sibley Manor on West Seventh Street. I was really excited about my new opportunity to get into coaching. I was also excited about the fact that I was only about a year away from completing my degree. So, I took a full schedule of classes as well. Being on campus was a lot of fun and I had a ball as the freshman coach of the Gophers. The only downside of being back in Minnesota was the fact that John wasn't around very much at the time. You see, he had been named as the head coach of the 1956 U.S. Olympic team that would ultimately win a silver medal in Cortina, Italy. So, he would come by, but not on a daily basis.

Instead, Marsh Ryman, who would later serve as the University's long-time athletics director, had been named as the interim coach and I would work under him. It was a good bunch of kids. Freshman weren't eligible to play in those days, so we had some really good players. Among them was a fiery kid by the name of Herbie Brooks, who would later become the program's most successful coach of all time. He would also become a very dear friend of mine and someone I really admired. He was a fantastic player, really fast and really smart. I knew he was going to be special.

I used to travel with the varsity and serve as an assistant to Marsh as well. We had some good players on the varsity team that year, guys like Ken Yackel, Jack McCartan, Dick Burg, Marv Jorde and Jack Petroske, to name a few. Now, Marsh was a feisty little guy. He didn't take any sh-- from anybody. He would get into arguments with the opposing team coaches and tell them that they needed us a lot more than we needed them, and would threaten to never come back and play them again if they didn't take care of whatever he was bitching about. Our players used to come to me and just shake their heads at this stuff. Before long the players had their own secret nickname for Marsh, "Ruhtracam" (pronounced: Roo-track-em). Eventually Marsh came up to me and asked me privately just what the hell the nickname meant, because he didn't have any idea. So, I went to one of the players and he explained to me that it was MacArthur spelled backwards, as in General MacArthur. It was MacArthur whose famous last words were "I shall return," and Marsh was the polar opposite of that. Everywhere we went he would tell them that they were a bunch of no good sons of bitches and that we were never coming back. It was cute, I got a kick out of it. I never had the heart to tell Marsh what it really meant though, but I did finally explain it to him about 20 years later. We both had a good laugh over that one.

I will never forget one time when we were

Bun Cook, Wally Hergesheimer, me & Eric Pogue

playing a game at the old Chicago Stadium. It was just before the game was to start and somebody came up to tell Marsh that he had an important phone call waiting for him. So, we both ran down to the office of the Blackhawk's general manager, Bill Tobin, to see what it was all about. Well, it was Mariucci, who was out in Boston at the time playing an exhibition game with the U.S. Olympic team. They hadn't headed overseas yet. He tells Marsh that they just lost one of his top defenseman to an injury and he wanted to invite Jack Petroske to join the Olympic team. So, we went and got Jack and told him the news. He was so excited about it and got really emotional.

It was at that time that I realized just how special it was for American kids to be able to play on their U.S. Olympic teams. You see, in Canada as kids we grew up dreaming of winning Stanley Cups, not winning gold medals. But in America, where just a handful of kids had ever played in the National Hockey League at that point in history, it was all about the Olympics. That was the pinnacle for them and I never understood that until that very moment. I saw how much it meant to him and that really stuck with me. Anyway, it was a great honor for Jack and we were very happy for him. Marsh was so tickled for Jack that he actually threw poor Bill Tobin right out of his own office so that we could celebrate the good news. It was hilarious.

Well, the Gophers had a good season and I learned a lot about what it takes to become a coach. I worked hard that year and was very

ONE FOR GLEN

In a pre-game ceremony, Mrs. Glen Sonmor throws out puck between Pittsburgh center Bob Bailey, left, and Captain Jackie Gordon of the Barons prior to last night's benefit game for Glen Sonmor, the Barons' injured player still confined in a Pittsburgh hospital. Over 7,700 fans filled the Arena and $8,7__ was paid into the boxoffice to aid Sonmor. (Photos by News Photographer B__ Nehez.)

The opening face-off for my benefit game in Cleveland

proud to be able to graduate with distinction from the University in the Spring of 1956 with a degree in physical education. By now John had been back from Italy and he wanted me to stay with him so that we could coach together. I thought about it and considered getting my masters degree, but I was restless. At that point, the owner of the Cleveland Barons had lined me up a job working at his bank. I was a hot-shot college graduate and figured I would give it a try. So, we headed back to Cleveland, where I was informed that I was going to have to learn the business from the bottom up — starting in the collections department.

I will never forget going out on my first call to pick up a payment from this Chinese family. I got there and the wife had kids hanging all over her and the husband was out in the garage trying to repair some old radios. He was trying to do some odd jobs in order to scrape a few bucks together. He was a really nice fellow, he had just fallen on some hard times. He told me his troubles and I just felt awful for him. So, instead of leaning on him to make him pay the bank, I took out my wallet and gave the poor guy the only $20 bucks I had on me. Needless to say, I didn't last very long in the world of finance.

From there, the team owner lined me up with another job back up in St. Catharines, Ontario, about 45 minutes from Hamilton. I would be working for a company called Thompson Products in their public relations department. In addition, I would also be coaching their Junior B team that they sponsored, the Teepees (named for their initials T.P.) which were a Blackhawks affiliate. I told my boss that I wanted to get into coaching and he really helped me out. Our daughter was two years old at the time and my wife and I were really excited about getting back to Hamilton. It was there where we put that nest egg money from the charity game to good use, when we purchased our first home, a lovely brick rambler that cost about $12 grand.

As the coach of the Teepees, I would follow Rudy Pilous, who had just led the team to a Memorial Cup championship the year before. Rudy got called up to coach in Chicago, so I was brought in to take over the Teepees. Rudy was a control freak and we bucked heads from day one. He still wanted to micromanage the team from Chicago and it was tough. It was fun to coach the team though. Guys like Stan Mikita, Denis DeJordy, John McKenzie and Wayne Hillman were all on the roster. Bobby Hull, the future Hall of Famer, was going to be our star player, but got called up to Chicago after rifling in a couple of goals during a training-camp exhibition game. The team went on to finish in first place in our division but then lost to the Toronto Marlboros in the Memorial Cup Playoffs. We played well, but I was ready to move on. Rudy and I didn't get along and I didn't want to wait around for him to fire me. So, I put out the feelers to test the waters.

Ch. 4 Old Blood & Guts...

With that, I called my father-in-law and had him put out the word that I was looking for a job. My father-in-law was a guy by the name of Johnny Mitchell, who was a well known hockey man in Canada at the time. He had worked with several NHL teams as a scout, including the Detroit Red Wings, and knew a lot of people. Incidentally, he had also been the general manager of the famed Johnstown Jets as well. In fact, the actor Strother Martin played his character in the classic movie "Slapshot." It was actually his office at the rink where they shot the movie, so that was kind of a fun tid-bit too.

Anyway, a few weeks later I got a call from none other than Eddie Shore, the former Boston Bruins Hall of Fame defenseman. He wanted to talk to me about coaching his Springfield Indians team that he owned in the American Hockey League. I was floored. I just couldn't believe that this guy was calling me. Eddie was in town scouting so I went and met with him at his hotel. He loved the fact that I had gotten into some pretty good brawls as a player and believe it or not, that was mostly what he wanted to talk about. It was funny, he didn't ask me one thing about any coaching strategy or anything like that, he just wanted to talk about some old fights that he had seen me in. I used to have some epic battles with one of his toughest guys, Ross Lowe, and he wanted to hear all about how I had beaten him. He was an odd duck, old Eddie, but I was in awe of the guy. I mean before Doug Harvey and Bobby Orr, whenever they discussed an all-time NHL All-Star team, it was Shore at one point and an argument about who might be the second-best defenseman of all-time at the other. He was just that good.

Eddie Shore

Well, he wound up offering me the job and I took it. I was a bit hesitant because Eddie had a reputation for being a real tough S.O.B. Old "blood and guts," as he was know, he was a real beauty. He was known as a guy who was very tough to work for, a real tyrant, but I needed to prove myself on a bigger stage and thought that this was going to be a good opportunity for me. I figured that if I could succeed working with him, then I would have bigger and better coaching opportunities down the road. Plus, Eddie was a brilliant hockey tactician and I was anxious to learn as much as I could from him. I mean he had his guys practicing the Soviet's skating drills at a time when no one respected the Soviets, so he knew what he was doing.

With that, we packed up and moved to Massachusetts. I was excited about the opportunity and even more excited when I found out that Eddie had hired Johnny to serve as the team's general manager. You see, Eddie was in poor health at the time and needed some help in the front office. His doctor had told him to stay away from the rink for a while and avoid any stress. I could tell it was going to be a disaster right away because Eddie was one of those guys who liked to do everything himself and he liked it done exactly his own way. I figured I would do my best and stick it out for at least a season. After all, I was only about 28 years old at this point and it was a pretty big deal to be coaching in the AHL.

I got acquainted with the players and dove in head first, learning as I went. We had a good team but we were soft in goal. It was a big problem. We actually had another goalie who was pretty good, but he was up in Calgary at the time. His name was Hank Bassen. Hank had been playing on our affiliate team up there and Johnny and I wanted to sign him in the worst way. The kid was holding out over a measly $400 contract dispute for some reason or another though and Eddie wouldn't pay him. Eddie was really cheap and he used to do all sorts of crazy things that he thought would motivate his players. For instance, he would hold out on paying guys if he wasn't happy with the way they were playing. It was insane. And, it was probably illegal.

Anyway, he and this kid had some words and Eddie got pissed off. Well, Eddie was so stubborn and principled, once you crossed him he wasn't going to budge, no matter what. I remember Johnny and I taking Eddie to lunch to practically beg him to let us sign this kid and get him into camp. The kid was good, in fact he would go on to play in the NHL for many years. I remember at lunch Eddie finally got ticked at Johnny and said in his squeaky voice "Mr. Bassen will sit on his ass until he barks like a fox...". Eddie had this bizarre way of expressing himself and that was his way of saying no f---ing way. Johnny kept after him though and eventually convinced the old man to sign him midway through the season. Then, the crazy thing with that was that once he finally reported to the team, Eddie held him out for a few weeks while he tried to re-teach him how to play goalie what he called the "right way." It drove us all nuts. In fact, it ultimately cost us a chance to make the playoffs. But, Eddie just had to do things his own way, no matter what.

Coaching in Springfield was a trip, let me tell ya. Despite having to deal with Eddie's antics, I did have a pretty good time. We had a good team with a whole bunch of good players. We were tough too. In fact, Don Cherry was on that team, what a great guy. He of course would go on to coach the Boston Bruins and later become a legend in broadcasting as the famed host of "Hockey Night in Canada." I was able to try some new things as a coach and was enjoying the fact that even though I could no longer play the game, I could still be competitive as a coach. That was great for my personal morale.

Now, because Eddie had been in poor health at the time, he

would stay away from the rink and just let me do my thing out there. Well, he finally got better and with that he started coming to practices and what not. He just made life miserable for me at that point, it was brutal. He was such a control freak out there and really drove me nuts. I remember one time before practice I was out on the ice taking some wrist shots on goal. He came over and pointed that old crook of a finger at me and said "Mr. Sonmor...", he called you "Mr." when you were in trouble. "Mr. Sonmor," he says, "what in the hell are you doing?" I told him I was just out taking some wrist shots to get loosened up for practice. He then proceeds to lecture me for a half an hour about the proper technique on how to take a goddamn wrist shot. I couldn't believe it. He broke down my entire stance and grip and just read me the riot act about how I was doing it incorrectly and that my incompetence could lead to the players doing the same. He basically forbade me from taking any more shots in practice. I couldn't believe my ears, I thought this guy was nuts. I didn't want to make any waves though, so I just shook my head and kept my mouth shut. From there on out though, I used to have one of my players sit on look-out for him before practices so that I could skate around out there and take my wrist shots in peace.

Eddie's improving health made my life a living hell. I even half-heartedly joked about re-injuring him so that he would have to stay away for a while. He would come down to the rink and just undermine my ability to coach effectively by blowing his damn whistle all the time from the stands. He had this thing where whenever he blew his whistle the players had to immediately stop right where they were at so that he could yell at them about this or that. In fact, he would always pick out one person to holler at about how they were in the wrong position or were doing something wrong. I eventually tried to have fun with it and guess which player he was going to yell at. I would play this little game with myself to make the time pass by guessing which guy Eddie was going to get after for screwing up. I was never right once. It was always somebody else. He would blow his whistle and point that old crooked finger at some unsuspecting kid and let him have it. The poor kid wouldn't even know why he was getting his ass chewed for God sakes. The players used to just dread practices when he was around. That was Eddie. He was a real dandy.

"Coach" Sonmor

Eventually I knew that I was only going to stay for one season in Springfield. There was no way I could stay any longer than that, otherwise I might have gone insane. I remember being at a practice late that season and Eddie came over to me. He says "Mr. Sonmor, you have a whistle too. You're the captain of this ship, why don't you blow it once in a while?" By now I knew I wasn't coming back, so I let old Eddie have it. I said "I would Eddie, but you blow your f---ing whistle every 10 seconds, so when the hell am I going to have time to blow mine?" He whacked me on the top of my head after that and said "One of us must be crazy, and it must be me." He was something else, let me tell you.

Eddie was so damn cheap. Instead of hiring a maintenance guy to fix things, he would just as soon do everything himself. He would be up on a ladder fixing light bulbs in the rink; he would fix the toilets when they got clogged; he would be out on the tractor shoveling snow in the parking lot; he would just do it all. He also thought that he was a doctor if you can believe that. I remember one time one of our star players, Billy McCreary, wasn't feeling well. It was just before game-time and he looked awful. So, I went to go tell Eddie that I was going to let him sit out that night. You always had to clear everything like that with the old man, no matter what. Well, sure enough, once I told him about Billy he looks at me all suspicious and says "Mr. Sonmor, let me see him...". So, he heads down to the dressing room and walks right over to McCreary, who was sitting there in his long underwear about ready to pass out. Eddie comes over to him, doesn't ask him how he is doing or anything, and says "Mr. McCreary, stick out your tongue." Billy looks over at me and I just shrugged my shoulders. He then sticks out his tongue and Eddie gets right up in there and starts looking down his throat. He then stands up and says very confidently, "it's your liver." That was it. He then turned around and walked out of the room. All of the guys turned towards me and I just threw my hands up in the air and said "you heard the man, it must be his liver!" We all had a good laugh over that one.

The guys were always in horror of Eddie trying to administer medical care to them. If they were sick or if they had an injury, they would try to hide it from him. Eddie was so cheap that he figured he could fix whatever it was for a heck of a lot less money than some fancy doctor could. Back problems were the worst. If a player had a bad back it was all over. Once Eddie got wind of that he would march into the locker room and grab that guy and throw him on the training table so he could go to work on him. He couldn't wait. He thought that he was a chiropractor, he really did. He would get up on the table and start putting his knees and elbows all over the place. The unfortunate player with the bad back had to just lay there, humiliated, and endure the torture for fear he would get his paycheck docked if the refused.

More often than not I am sure he caused more damage to them than what they started with. I will never forget poor Bob McCord who made the mistake of letting Eddie see him hunched over with back pain one time. Sure enough, Shore threw him up on the table and went to work on him. Well, he screwed him up so bad that Bob couldn't even hold his head up for about a week after that. He was walking around like the Hunchback of Notre Dame after that. We eventually had to send him to see a specialist in Boston, it was unbelievable. Eventually the sh-

- disturbers in the locker room would have fun with it and whenever they would see Eddie come into the locker room they would shout out "Hey so-and-so, how's your bad back feeling?" Old Eddie's ears would perk up and the poor sap who got his name called out would just cringe. It was hilarious.

Eddie was such a control freak, he really was. He insisted that none of the players drank or smoke or anything like that. Then, on top of that, he would even call the player's wives in once a year to lecture them on how important it was for them to leave their husbands alone on the nights before games. He thought that if guys had sex before games that it would make them more relaxed and not very aggressive, so he forbade it. Unbelievable. He did allow them to drink once a year though. He would have an annual team party after a practice and he would bring in all sorts of booze for them. He would have beer, the hard stuff, and then some brandy for himself. That was his drink, brandy. Well, after a while a bunch of the players would get all liquored up and tell off old Eddie. He would be sitting in the corner sipping on his brandy and sure enough, someone would come over and start screaming "You rotten bald-headed mother-f---er!". The player would usually get fined, but they didn't care. It was worth it.

Years earlier one of the players told me a story that happened at one of the team parties when Eddie got just hammered and then went out afterwards with one of the players to a bar. Well, they got into some trouble and wound up in jail. Eddie had money and bailed himself out but refused to pay for the player, so he had to spend the night in the clink. Then, the next morning at practice, he had the audacity to fine the poor kid for being late. What a beauty!

Eventually, after that one year in Springfield, I lined up a teaching and coaching job back up in Hamilton at Westdale High School. I couldn't work for Eddie any more and wanted to have a more stable job for my family. My daughter was four years old at the time and was about to start school. So, I wanted to get settled and put down some roots back in our hometown. We were even able to move back into our house in St. Catharines because we were unable to sell it from when we had lived there the year before. At Westdale I taught physical education and coached both the varsity hockey team as well as the junior (9th & 10th graders) football team. My wife taught at a different school in Hamilton as well. We were both happy to be back and doing what we enjoyed.

The school's superintendent, Dr. Price, was my old ally from high school who had helped me out when I was having eligibility issues while playing junior hockey up in Guelph. Price saw how tough it was for kids like myself to have to move to those small towns in order to have a chance to play hockey at a higher level. As a result, many of the kids who want to play hockey wind up having to drop out of school, which is an unfortunate byproduct of Canada's youth and minor hockey programs. So, when I came to Westdale he put me in charge of running one of the country's first high school hockey programs. He was determined to give kids a chance to advance their hockey careers without having to leave home to play Junior hockey, and he succeeded. In fact, his two sons were on the team and both wound up getting college hockey scholarships to Harvard. I felt pretty good about that. We had some good hockey teams and I really enjoyed working with the kids at that level too, teaching them about playing the game the right way, with respect. I also tried to instill in them a strong work ethic, because I have always believed that there are no short cuts in life — it all comes down to hard work.

I was at Westdale for four years and then went to a new school called Southmount, where I was promoted to the head of the physical education department as an athletic director. I also coached the hockey team there as well. When I left Westdale, there was a ceremony in the school's auditorium on the last day of school. There, the principal announced the names of all of the teachers who weren't coming back the next year. When my name was announced the students started to applaud, and they wouldn't stop. They just kept clapping and clapping, it meant so much to me. Many of them had told me that I was their favorite teacher, and that was so rewarding.

Incidentally, the person who took over my old job at Westdale was a guy by the name of Harry Neale. Harry had originally graduated from the University of Toronto and had been teaching and coaching at another high school in Hamilton prior to that. We had coached against each other in football and hockey over the years and had gotten to know each other. So, I recommended him for the job at Westdale. Little did I know at the time, but it was the beginning of what would turn out to be a wonderful lifelong friendship.

During those summers I would take graduate course work, first at the Ontario College of Education, and later at Ohio State University. I wanted to get the best education possible and Ohio State had a fantastic physical education program. It was tough commuting to Columbus, Ohio, during the Summers, but I made the most of it. I would eventually just stay down there in an apartment. I went there for four straight Summers, it was a big commitment. I even had some fun coaching the Buckeyes club hockey team on the side and helped to turn that into a varsity program. That was fun too. We played a lot of the smaller schools throughout the Midwest and it was very rewarding to get that program up and running.

Well, we eventu-

Former American Hockey League star Glenn Sonmor has coached the Westdale Warriors high school team to four straight victories in the new Hamilton Interscholastic Hockey League. The Warriors won their fourth game without a defeat earlier this week, when they dumped Central, 5-2. Here, Sonmor rehashes the recent win with John Price, (right) and Ron Wilson.

Coaching at Westdale High School

ally bought a new house in Ancaster, just outside of Hamilton. Things were going well. However, it was at about this time that I think I started to have some problems with alcohol. I had a lot of time on my hands and before long I was starting to abuse it. I had always drank beer with my teammates and occasionally had gotten drunk from time to time, but it wasn't a problem early on. I think that was because I was so busy and so determined to succeed. Once I slowed down a little bit, it began to take a hold of me. And, when I was off to Ohio by myself, it gave me plenty of time to drink with the guys and kick up my heels. It wasn't serious at that point, but it was probably the beginning of my problems with the disease as I look back now.

By 1966 I had nearly finished all of my coursework needed towards obtaining my masters degree. I was just a couple of classes short. I knew that if I was going to coach at the college level then I would need to have my masters, it was really important for me to get it. That's when I got another phone call from my old friend John Mariucci, who told me that I was his choice to succeed him as the head coach at the University of Minnesota. I nearly dropped the phone. John was leaving the University to join the front office of the NHL's newest expansion team, the Minnesota North Stars, which were to begin the following year in 1967. He told me that he had gone to the Gopher athletic department and told them that I was his choice for the job and that he wouldn't take no for an answer. Marsh Ryman, who I coached under several years earlier, was the University's athletics director by this point and he really liked me. So, the job was mine if I wanted it. And, as if that weren't enough, they told me that I wouldn't need to have a masters degree to get the job. I could hardly contain myself I was so excited.

John Mariucci

Ch. 5
Back to Gold Country...

The next thing I knew we were packing our belongings and moving back to the Land of 10,000 Lakes. We got a place across from the Southdale Mall. I was really excited about my new job and about the opportunities that were ahead of me. I couldn't wait to get down to Williams Arena and get situated. As for my outlook, I would inherit a pretty decent team. Mariucci had led the team to a 16-11 overall record in 1965-66, good for second place in the WCHA. My staff was pretty bare-boned, but I did have an outstanding freshman coach — a kid by the name of Louie Nanne. Louie was coming off an All-America career with the Gophers and was getting ready to play on the U.S. Olympic team over in Grenoble, France. We hit it off right away, I just loved him. Little did I know, however, that it would be the beginning a wonderful lifelong friendship that has spanned more than 40 years now.

I wound up sharing an office in Cook Hall with Dick Siebert, the legendary Gopher baseball coach, and Les Bolstad, the longtime Gopher golf coach. What a treat that was to share stories with those two guys. Both were wonderful men and I learned a great deal about coaching from them. It was a real break for me to be in there with those guys, it really was. They were wonderful mentors for me as I was just getting started in my coaching career. Being back on campus was a lot of fun. Just to be around that environment, with all of the students and what not, was so energizing to me. I was really motivated to jump in and start coaching. I wanted like hell to win some games and to make a name for myself. I had some pretty big shoes to fill, but felt like I was up for the challenge.

Our team had some talent. Jack Dale would lead the squad with 43 points, while Denny Zacho, Gary Gambucci, Dick Paradise and Chuck Norby would all contribute a great deal as well. There was also the great line from St. Paul Johnson: Mike Crupi, Rob Shattuck and Greg Hughes, those guys were great. We were thin in goal though and that hurt us all year. We had a fantastic goaltender, Murray McLachlan, who was a freshman and therefore couldn't play on the varsity. In fact, that season was the last year that freshman weren't allowed to play with the varsity. Unfortunately, it was a year too late and we had to take our lumps as we finished with an overall record of 9-

The Old Barn

19-1. We wound up going with two goaltenders, Peter Roussopoulos and Mike Lechtman, and both of them struggled whenever they would let in a goal. So, I finally told them that I was going to rotate them after every goal that was scored, and that was what we did. Neither was too thrilled about it, but I just felt like that was the best way to handle the situation. The guys still rib me about that all these years later.

I got a lot of help recruiting that season from Mariucci, as well as from boosters like George Lyon and Bruce Telander. Those guys were really connected and that helped me out a lot. They were all tied into the local Junior hockey circuit, which was just beginning around here. They would all prove to be invaluable for me. You know, John always stressed the high school players, and the importance of the Minnesota players in particular. He wanted to give them a chance. Sure, if there were some great Canadian kids who could contribute, he would never shy away from them. But he really wanted the local kids to get a shot at the University if they so desired. I followed that advice and it would serve me well. The Minnesota high school hockey tournament was such a big deal in those days and there was so much talent coming out of here that I didn't need to look anywhere else to tell you the truth.

That next year our new goalie, Murray McLachlan, really carried us. He was as good as anybody in the country. He would turn out to be our MVP for three straight years and was just a fabulous player. Gambucci played great that next season too, as did Bill Klatt, Pete Fichuk, Pat Westrum and Greg Hughes. We improved a great deal, finishing with a 19-12 record and a fifth place conference finish. Gambucci earned All-American honors, which was really special for all of us too. We finished in fifth again that following year and wound up losing to Michigan out in Ann Arbor in the WCHA Playoffs. It was neat to make it to the post-season, but I wanted so much more out of my guys and out of myself.

John Mariucci & John Mayasich

It all finally came together for us in 1969-70 though. That was the year we really made a splash. Wally Olds and McLachlin were both named as All-Americans, which was really neat. We were led in scoring that year by a kid by the name of Mike Antonovich, an Iron Ranger from Greenway who I absolutely fell in love with. In fact, to this day he is my absolute favorite player that I have ever coached at any level. What a fantastic player. He wasn't very big, but he was faster than hell and really tough. I will never forget when some of our recruiters started to talk about him and about how he was going to be the savior of the program. I went to check him out at a local junior game the summer before he got here and I couldn't believe my eyes. First of all, he was just a little guy — maybe five-foot-four at the most, and about a buck thirty soaking wet. I thought those guys must be nuts. But then, when I saw him play, I knew that he was going to be something special. He, along with Dean Blais, Ron Peltier, Craig Sarner, Mike Kurtz and of course our top defenseman, Wally Olds, really played some great hockey for us that season. McLachlan was so strong in goal for us too and we really gelled together as a team. We wound up winning the WCHA title with an overall record of 21-12-0 and I was even named as the WCHA Coach of the Year as well, which meant a lot to me.

Another fun thing happened that year as well just before Christmas when we hosted the Big Ten Tournament at Williams Arena and wound up beating Ohio State, 4-0. What was significant about that was the fact that the coach of that Buckeye team was my old buddy, Harry Neale. You see, Harry had followed me at Ohio State and taken over the program when I left to come to Minnesota. I will never forget when he got here, he walked right into my office and started re-arranging all the furniture, telling me how it would look when he followed me here too. It was hilarious. We both had a great laugh over that one. Harry, of course, would later go on to coach in the NHL and later serve as the voice of "Hockey Night in Canada."

I will never forget beating Duluth in a double-overtime thriller in the opening round of the WCHA playoffs. Mike Antonovich ended it for us, what a great game that was. I remember kind of a funny incident that happened during another game up there one time the year before with Anonovich. You see, I was always telling the guys to play tough and to be physical by finishing their checks and sticking up for each other out on the ice. Well, there was this one Duluth fan who always sat in the same spot and gave the opposing players hell all game. Well, during the game this loudmouth reached over and grabbed Antonovich's stick when he was checked over by the boards near him. Now, I was looking for an excuse to nail this idiot, and figured this would be as close as I would get.

So, I jumped up from the bench, ran over to him across the ice and beat the snot out of the guy. I knew he wasn't a fighter because he just kept grabbing my shirt, while I bloodied his face. My assistant coach at the time, Herbie Brooks, even came running down to my defense from the press-box. When they finally got me off of the guy all I was wearing was a tie. My jacket and shirt were all torn off of me. I must have been quite a sight. I guess I showed that drunk

Herbie Brooks

SHIRLEY WAS ON THE ICE 45

son-of-a-bitch a thing or two about messing with a Gopher though! After the game I got up on a table in the locker room and waved that torn shirt around like a victory flag. It was something else, let me tell you. Unfortunately we couldn't capitalize on that momentum though because we wound up losing the next night to Michigan Tech, 6-5, to end the season.

You know, one of the biggest catalysts that got us going that season came shortly after I had to cut two kids from the team, Jim Ebbitt and Rich Urich. I just didn't feel like they were fitting in at the time. It was tough, but I felt very strongly about the importance of team chemistry. They were on a line with Dean Blais, one of my top freshmen players, and I felt like their bad attitudes might rub off on him. So, one day I had my trainer, Jimmy Marshall, call them into my office before practice. One by one they came in and I told them what was happening. Each one would leave and then return to the locker room, whereupon he would immediately start to clean out his locker. Finally, after both guys are cleaning out their lockers, I called Dean into my office.

By now the entire team knows what is going on and they are all terrified that I had gone nuts or something. Well, Dean comes into my office with eyes about as big as saucers, wondering if he was next on the chopping block. I was going to string him out, but I didn't want him to have a heart attack right there in my office. So I told him that he was just fine and that I had done what I felt was the best thing for the team and for his development. Even to this day, whenever I see Dean we laugh about that. It was a light moment in what would prove to be one of my toughest days as a coach. It was never easy cutting guys, but those are the things you have to do sometimes for the good of the team.

Another funny thing that happened after that came when Murray McLachlan approached me and wondered if his status on the team was all right. You see, both of the guys I cut were Canadian, as was Murray, and he wondered if I was cleaning house or something and just going with Minnesota kids. Me, being a proud Canadian as well, assured him that everything was all right and that he had nothing to worry about. I told him that it wouldn't have mattered if those guys were from Antarctica, they just had to go. I wanted to win and I wasn't going to tolerate players who weren't going to give it their all and put the team first. They were good kids, but just didn't fit into what I wanted to do at the time. I didn't pull their scholarships or anything either, I just wanted to go in a different direction. Looking back, it was probably just the wake-up call that our team needed to come together and start playing some inspired hockey.

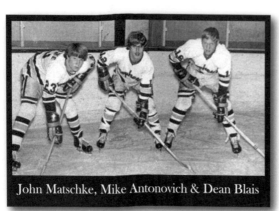

John Matschke, Mike Antonovich & Dean Blais

While we had a

great year in 1969-70, it even got better in 1970-71, when we made it all the way to the NCAA Final Four championship game. That was such an entertaining team. Our top line was Mike Antonovich, Dean Blais and Johnny Matschke. Our second line featured the two Peltier brothers, Ron and Doug, along with Craig Sarner. Then, our third group was an all-freshman line of Jimmy Gambucci, Bruce Carlson and John Harris — who would go on to become a world class golfer. Wally Olds and Bruce McIntosh were our star defenseman, while Dennis Erickson and Brad Shelstad played solid in goal.

The crowds were coming out like crazy to see us at Williams Arena — what a fantastic place to watch a hockey game. We had some great rivalries with Wisconsin in those days and even set the attendance record during one tough series with those bastards. It was great. I couldn't stand "Badger" Bob Johnson and made no bones about that. We both started coaching together in the WCHA at about the same time and didn't like each other. Our teams shared that same sentiment. We had a hell of a rivalry with those guys and had some epic battles with them over the years.

Anyway, we had only finished with a 14-17-2 overall record, good for just fifth in the conference. But we got hot at the end of the year and made a nice run. We ultimately finished with runner-up honors at the NCAA Finals, where we lost a very close game to Boston University, 4-2. We beat Wisconsin and North Dakota in the WCHA Playoffs and then got past Harvard in the semifinals, 6-5, in overtime, out in Syracuse, NY. We were down 5-4 late in this game against the Crimson and we got a penalty. Well, I never believed in protecting a loss, so I pulled our goalie with a minute or so to go in the game. Dean Blais was able to come up with the puck deep in their end and then find Johnny Matschke out in front of the net with just a few seconds left on the clock. Johnny knew what to do with the puck and he buried it to send it to overtime. Then, in sudden-death, Ron Peltier got the game-winner to send us to the Finals. It was a marvelous game, it really was.

Then, in the Finals, we lost to BU by the final of 4-2. I remember our goalie, Dennis Erickson, getting hit with a puck right square in the knee cap early in the game. He wore these dinky little leg pads for some reason. I was always telling him to get bigger ones, but that was what he was comfortable with and what he wanted to wear. So, our trainer, Jimmy Marshall sprayed some of that Novocain stuff on his knee to freeze it so he could get back into the game. He was hobbling around out there and clearly

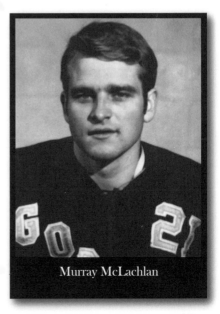

Murray McLachlan

47

was not himself. I didn't want to put Shelstad in the game though because he was only a freshman. I stuck with Erickson and he did his best, but we came up short. Incredibly, when we got back to Minneapolis, Erickson went in for X-rays and it turned out that he had played 52 minutes with a broken knee cap. I felt just awful. Losing that game was really tough though. It was as close as I would ever get to winning an NCAA championship and I was really bummed out that it never happened for me. I wanted it for the fans so badly, they were really with us that year.

The next season would prove to be a wild one for me. It started out pretty rough and we lost a bunch of games right out of the gate. We had lost a bunch of guys to graduation and to the pros, but we had a solid roster of players that I had felt pretty good about being able to rebuild with. I figured we would get it worked out, but then I got a phone call that changed everything. You see, things started to become interesting for me earlier in the year when it had been announced that there was a new franchise coming to town from the upstart World Hockey Association.

The WHA was a rebel league that was going to compete directly with the NHL. The ownership groups were setting up their front offices in preparation of the league starting that next year, and I was contacted by the group from the Minnesota Fighting Saints about becoming their head coach. Several Twin Cities businessmen with ties to local hockey, including Lou Kaplan, Frank Marzitelli and Len Vannelli were involved, and they were familiar with me and my coaching style. They had already started building the Civic Center in downtown St. Paul, where the team was going to be based out of, and it was a pretty exciting time.

I was happy being the head coach of the Gophers, but when the Saints' ownership group made me an offer to run the team's hockey operations as both the general manager and coach, I couldn't turn it down. It had always been a dream of mine to coach in the NHL, and I figured

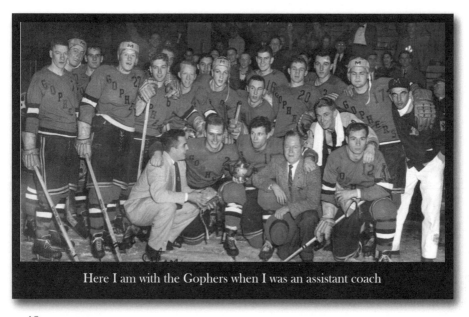

Here I am with the Gophers when I was an assistant coach

that this was going to be a great opportunity for me to be able to get closer to achieving that goal. I am a competitive person and wanted to experience a new challenge too. I wanted to see how I would do at that level, so that was also a big factor in my decision to ultimately leave the team midway through that season.

So, that November I went to see my old friend, Paul Giel, who had recently been named as the University's athletics director, to tell him that I was going to be leaving. The Saints were going to start playing in October of 1972, so I had about 11 months to hire a coaching staff and assemble a team. It was going to be crazy and I was going to have to do a whole bunch of traveling over the ensuing months. So, I told Paul that I wanted to leave midway through the season, but at the same time I didn't want to leave him in a bind. He was great about it though and encouraged me to follow my heart. I really appreciated that. We had gone to school together and had become good friends. He was such an amazing athlete when he was with the Gophers, both in football and in baseball, and to see him get the job as the A.D. was just wonderful. I was so sad when Paul died a few years back in 2002, what a wonderful person he was.

So, I left the team in December of 1971 and was replaced by Kenny Yackel. Paul and I figured that that would be the best way to go. Yack was a good guy. He was a hell of an athlete at the University and was running some hockey schools at the time, in addition to running a very successful insurance business. We were glad that he was able to help us out. He would remain as the interim coach for the rest of the season until Herbie Brooks could take over the next year. That played into it too, knowing that Herbie was in line to take over the program. He came in to be my freshman coach a short while after Louie Nanne left to join the North Stars in '68 and I knew that he would be perfect for the job. I think back now to my role in Gopher hockey as the bridge between John Mariucci and Herb Brooks, two legends in the world of hockey.

Truth be told, we offered Herbie the job to take over for me right away but he said that he couldn't. You see, he was selling insurance at the time on the side and had made a commitment to them. So, he turned it down and said that he could start the following season, but not right then. I mean here is a guy who dreamed of coaching at the Division One level, at his alma mater nonetheless, yet turned it down because he wanted to keep his word to an insurance company. Wow. That was amazing to me, but a real testament to just how loyal he really was. I really respected that about him. So, we let him do it and we brought in Yackel to finish the season. We knew that Herbie was going to be a great one, there was just something about him. The players really looked up to him. We were

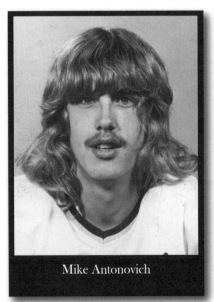

Mike Antonovich

polar opposites as coaches too. I was always B.S.'ing around with the players and having fun with them, whereas Herbie was much tougher on them and just kept to himself. He had his own unique style, that was for. Looking back now, and realizing that he would go on to win three national championships from 1972-79 and turn the Gopher program into a national dynasty, I think we made the right decision.

You know, when I think back to working with Herbie in those days, it was a lot of fun. He was so principled and stubborn, even back then. I will never forget the time we were going to the NCAA Finals in 1971 and Marsh Ryman, the athletics director, told me that he didn't have it in the budget for us to be able to take Herbie along. I never told Herbie about it though. I just went to a couple of our boosters, who gave me the money on the side. But, when Herbie somehow found out about that he said to hell with it. He was so upset over the fact that Marsh didn't think his role on the team was important enough for him to go that he refused to go even when we did have a ticket for him. I was upset because he was my only assistant coach, but he just wouldn't budge. That was Herbie.

All in all, I had a fantastic time coaching the Gophers. It was a great experience for me. I loved being on campus and going to football games and just being around that college atmosphere. I loved coaching at that level too, because you could really have an impact on the kids at that age. I was a teacher, and I loved teaching. Coaching college kids was a real joy because the student-athletes are there in an educational setting and are very open to learning new things. It wasn't like coaching the Junior players up in Canada, who were in a totally different mind set and focused solely on getting on to the pros.

You know, in those days the coaches all taught physical education classes on the side, so that was a lot of fun too. I remember coaching a softball class one time and getting drilled right in the nose with a line drive. My nose got busted up and was just a bloody mess. I wanted to show the kids how tough I was though, so I just walked right over to the clinic and got it fixed up like nothing had happened. I had some great kids and some great assistant coaches in those years. In addition to Louie and Herbie, I also had Tom Saterdahlen as a coach too. Tom was a great guy and would go on to become one of the winningest coaches in Minnesota state high school hockey history at Bloomington Jefferson.

To be honest, I was sad to go in many regards. I had been going to school at the University since 1949, when John Mariucci had gotten me

Here is my transcript from the University of Minnesota, a real prized possession...

enrolled by the scuff of my neck. Then, when I was with Cleveland and even with New York, I would come back during the Summers to take Summer school. I finally got my degree in 1967, but took graduate courses even when I was coaching. I just loved learning about new and different things and to be in that type of environment. So, it was bitter-sweet to leave the University of Minnesota. I will always be a Gopher though, that is for sure. I can honestly say that I truly do bleed Maroon and Gold.

Now, this is a good place to interject and talk about what was going on in my personal life at the time. It would be safe to say that I had been drinking too much at this point in my life, no question. I was never an everyday drinker, or what might be termed as a chronic drinker. Rather, I was a spree drinker or binge drinker, and would get into trouble after drinking too much at one sitting. I was hanging out with all my hockey buddies, including John Mariucci, and having some good times. My first big problem came in 1970 when I had gotten arrested for drunk driving. The story got out in the newspapers and it was very embarrassing. I knew that I could lose my job if I didn't shape up, so I got sober for about a year after that. I even started going to some sobriety meetings, like many alcoholics do, but I wasn't ready to get cured. So, I started to sneak around after that in order to continue my drinking. I was in denial and didn't think that I had a problem. We go through stages, those of us who battle this disease, and I was not convinced yet that I couldn't drink.

All of the traveling associated with hockey made it tough too. When you are on the road so much, playing on weekends, or recruiting, it affords you a lot of time to get into trouble. I remember going on a scouting trip up to the Iron Range one time and wound up staying in a hotel for a few days longer than I needed to. I would just hang out up there and drink. I was in this hotel in Grand Rapids and hung around the

Mariucci, yours truly, Doc Romnes & Herbie — all former Gopher coaches

bar, where I would get drunk and try to chase around a bit, which usually went hand in hand when you were drinking. Luckily for me, I was not a very smooth operator when it came to picking up gals at hotel bars though. Again, I am not proud of that in any way. But, it was what it was, and I need to be honest about that.

I would find reasons to stay in hotels for a few extra days here and there and would find excuses for it. If I didn't have a reason, then I would make one up. I would rationalize it and justify it to myself. Luckily, I had guys like Glen Gostick, one of the team trainers who also taught phys-ed classes, back in the office covering my for me. I had people all over covering for me and unknowingly enabling me to do what I was doing. I feel very badly about that now, I really do. Anyway, I was drinking too much and staying out too late. I didn't feel like it was a big problem at the time though, because I was busy and had a lot of ambition with my career. I think that as soon as you aren't ambitious in life, and have some free time on your hands, that is when you can really fall fast into the depths of alcoholism. My situation was unique, but it was a problem that seemed to grow bigger and bigger at every turn.

To make matters worse, my wife and I were having troubles at this point as well. In fact, we both knew that our marriage was coming to an end. Certainly my addiction to alcohol was a major factor in that turn of events. I was sad though because I loved my daughter very much and didn't want to do anything that would upset her.

6 The Fighting Saints, Boy Were They Ever...

There was a big risk in me leaving my tenured teaching job with the Gophers and going to the WHA. I had job security and a pension at the University but was willing to take a gamble. That was my nature I suppose. I was only 42 years old at the time and was anxious to try my hand at something new. College hockey is so much different than professional hockey and I was limited as to just how much I could do tactically in that environment. I had posted what I would consider to be a pretty modest 78-80-6 record with the Gophers, but was ready for a new challenge. So, the timing was right. Plus, the fact that I didn't have to pack up and move or anything was also appealing to me as well.

OK, I think it is important to look at what was going on in the world of hockey at this point from a historical perspective. You see, the WHA was in direct competition with the NHL and they were doing whatever they could to raid their top players. They needed to make a splash and when they signed Bobby Hull to a $1 million contract, people stood up and took notice in a hurry. Money like that was unheard of at the time. The guys who launched the WHA, Gary Davidson and Dennis Murphy, were the same people who had started the American Basketball Association, and they knew how to make a splash. I knew that if they failed though, that I could be blackballed from ever getting to coach in the NHL. It was the same for the players too, we were all going to be in the same boat in that regard. So, it was a big risk. I was confident in my abilities though and just couldn't turn it down.

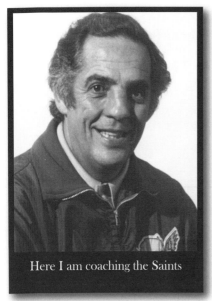

Here I am coaching the Saints

I remember hiring Ron Simon, a local attorney who I had gotten to know at the University, to work out the details of my contract. He represented me and made sure that it was all legit. I needed to know that I was going to get paid. I mean it wasn't like these guys from the WHA had a proven track record at that point or anything. I, like most people, was a little bit skeptical. Ron would later tell me that I was his first real client, so that is neat to think about too when you consider all of the famous athletes who he has represented over the years, from Kirby Puckett and Paul Molitor, on down the line. My contract called for a salary of $35 grand a year, which was double what I was making at the University. Back then that was a lot of money. I remember wondering to myself just how in the hell I would ever be able to spend it all.

After dotting the "i's" and crossed the "t's" on my contract, I jumped in and got to work. The first thing I did was to call my old buddy, Harry Neale, and hire him as my assistant coach. Harry had stayed on at Ohio State for four years and got that program going, but eventually got tired of trying to compete with the Buckeye's football and basketball coaches, Woody Hayes and Fred Taylor, who ran that campus and gobbled up all of the athletics budget. So, he finally said to hell with it and went back to Canada, where he ran some hockey schools. I was thrilled that he was available at the time and it was great to finally be able to work with him. He was such a smart guy and very respected in hockey circles. Plus, he had a lot of connections with the minor and Junior coaches up there, which was going to be a big help with regards to assembling our roster.

From there, we started combing the rosters of all the NHL teams and figuring out who we were going to go after. It was like a mad scramble at the time, it really was. It was an unprecedented time in hockey history. The NHL had recently expanded from six to 12 teams a few years earlier, and now there were going to be another 12 professional teams thrown into the fold. Guys were getting signed left and right, it was absolutely crazy. Some of the NHL teams had their entire minor league rosters depleted overnight. If you played hockey at that time and had a pulse, there was a good chance you were going to get a chance to play professionally at some level. Even if you weren't good enough to play in the top leagues, organizations now needed warm bodies to fill up their minor league teams which had just been emptied.

We both started pounding the pavement. I stayed in the States and focused on the American Hockey League and the college kids, while Harry scouted Canada. The AHL guys were only making around $15 or $20 grand a year at the time, so we could double that in order to get them to come play with us. We had so much to do in such little time. We needed to get the best players in here that we could, so that meant trying to recruit guys who were willing to leave for either more money or for more ice time. I remember going out to Oakland, to talk to the players on the Seals. That was the most disgruntled NHL franchise at the time and I figured that there would be a few top players out there who were pissed off enough at management to just say the hell with it and move to Minnesota. Sure enough, I was able to get a

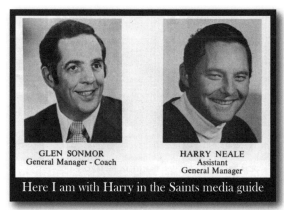

GLEN SONMOR
General Manager - Coach

HARRY NEALE
Assistant
General Manager

Here I am with Harry in the Saints media guide

55

couple of guys to jump ship. It felt kind of dirty, sneaking around like that to raid other team's rosters, but that was just how it was back then.

Now, because we didn't have a very big budget, I think our entire payroll was about $750,000 for a roster of 20 guys, we decided to go with as many local kids as we could. We figured that they would play here for less, and they would ultimately help us to sell tickets and fill up that big new arena. One of my first signees was my favorite player at the University, Mike Antonovich. In addition to being injured that year, he was having troubles playing for Yackel. We had very different coaching styles, Yack and I, and that was tough for him. Apparently, Yack had a rule where he would punish guys for swearing by making them do push-ups. Well, Antonovich, with his rough Iron Range vocabulary, started to look like Popeye from having to do so many push-ups that year. Plus, he wasn't that crazy about going to school. So, it all worked out and I was thrilled to get him on our roster. Lefty Curran, the outstanding goaltender from International Falls who would play on the 1972 U.S. Olympic team, was another guy we would get. Pretty soon the pieces of the puzzle all started to come together.

The league had a really glitzy draft in February of 1972 which was held out in California, complete with beautiful young girls who would take each team's selection and run it up to the big board — kind of like the gals who appear between rounds in a boxing match. It was quite a spectacle, really first class. There were hundreds of reporters there to cover it. I mean here was this brand new renegade league, challenging the long established NHL, and making a go if it. It was pretty neat. The guy behind it all was Bill Hunter, who was this really flamboyant guy who loved to hear himself talk. I will never forget when he got up in front of everybody to welcome them there and to kick off the festivities. The first words out of his mouth were: "Ladies and Gentlemen, this is the great-

Lefty Curran

est day in the history of the world!" I nearly wet my pants when I heard him say that. But, to his credit, he was a showman and really helped us get into the newspapers and on TV. We needed all the help we could get and he was out there making noise for us.

Now, everybody was fair game in the draft: players from the NHL, AHL, college kids, Olympians, Europeans or Junior players. We didn't know if guys would sign with us or not, but we could draft them nonetheless. There was a lottery to see which team would go first and low and behold, we got the first pick. So, the logical choice for us would be to take the most famous Minnesota player at the time, in order to start building our local fan base around him — Henry Boucha. Henry had become a high school legend up in Warroad and was just a fantastic player. What was funny about that moment though, was that when Hunter made his big announcement "The St. Paul Fighting Saints now have the first ever pick of the WHA draft...", we were supposed to have our gal run up there with this big card that had Henry's name on it. Hunter, meanwhile, had made name cards for what seemed like thousands of players. I mean he left no stone unturned in his quest to pull off this big gala without a hitch. He figured he had everybody's name who could possibly ever be drafted. Sure enough, we step up there and I had to tell him, "Bill, we don't have a name card for the No. 1 overall player in the draft." He couldn't believe it. The poor guy was just crushed. It was pretty hilarious.

Here is where it gets confusing. You see, Henry was already signed up to play for Murray Williamson's 1972 U.S. Olympic team, which would ultimately win a silver medal over in Sapporo, Japan. Murray, who is a great friend and somebody who I really respect in the hockey world, was in a predicament at the time. You see, the WHA had offered him the job to coach the franchise in Philadelphia, but the NHL stepped in and got him a job running a new Junior league here in Minnesota instead. They compensated him pretty handsomely and even gave him an office at the Met Center. They wanted to keep him away from us in a big way. There was all sorts of jockeying between the two leagues that was going on like this behind the scenes.

Basically, the NHL was fighting back any way that they could in order to prevent the WHA from drafting the top amateur players. It was war. The NHL quickly realized that we were for real, and knew that they had to do something to protect their interests. As a result, the NHL dug deep into their financial reserves and tried to tie-up a lot of their players to long-term contracts, to prevent them from being seduced by us. The WHA then responded with a variety of ploys to attract players. Among them included drafting 18-year-olds, instead of the NHL's then-draft age of 20. This infuriated the NHL GM's, who didn't want to gamble on the abilities of inexperienced kids. The NHL answered back by raising their own salaries, lowering their draft age eligibility, and even went as far as adding new franchises in strategic cities around the U.S. and Canada, including Atlanta and the N.Y. Islanders. It was a sort of "preemptive strike" to add even further competition and expense to the rival WHA teams which were going to be residing there.

The WHA also knew that they had to differentiate themselves

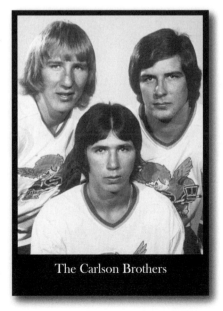

The Carlson Brothers

from the other guys in order to win over the fans. One of the things that they did was to allow their players to use big banana curves on their hockey stick blades. While the NHL allowed just a 1/2 inch curve, the WHA allowed a whopping 1 1/4 inches for its players to lift the puck into arena rafters. Another thing that they did was to use a different colored puck. Much like the old ABA used red, white and blue basketballs to separate themselves from the NBA, the WHA also wanted its own identity from the NHL. So, instead of using traditional black pucks, they decided to try a flaming red one. But, because the paint quickly peeled off of it, they went to blue instead. And, even though those proved to be soft and often bounced erratically on the ice, they became the signature trademark of the league.

Now, as for Henry Boucha, he ultimately wound up signing with the Detroit Red Wings instead of with us immediately following the Olympics. So, we were never able to sign him with that first overall pick. Incidentally, we did sign Henry a few years later in 1976, after he had made a comeback from his devastating eye injury that he suffered at the hands of Boston's Dave Forbes during a game when he was with the North Stars. Henry was fantastic with us too. He only wound up playing for one year, but he scored about a point per game. What a fantastic player, just pure, raw talent. He too was one of those guys who struggled with alcohol, and I could see that first hand when I was with him. Great guy though, I couldn't be happier that he eventually got his life straightened out.

When it was all said and done, we wound up with a lot of American guys on our roster. In fact, there were just 29 Americans in the entire league, and 10 of them were on our team that first year. About half of our roster included guys who had ties to Minnesota, including Mike Antonovich, Keith "Huffer" Christiansen, Craig Falkman, Jack McCar-

Pat Westrum

tan, Len Lilyholm, Dick Paradise and Bill Klatt. I remember we even had an open try-out for all Minnesota kids. It was sort of a publicity stunt to tell you the truth, because we figured that there was no way in hell that anybody who would have been good enough to play at that level would just roll in off of the street.

Well, sure enough, these three big lugs from Virginia, up on the Iron Range, came in and immediately caught our attention, the Carlson brothers — Jack, Jeff and Steve. They were something else. They were fresh out of high school and were playing Juniors at the time. Man, they were tough. I just loved those guys. They weren't good enough to play with us at that point, so we sent them off to one of our minor league affiliates in Marquette. They tore it up there, so we moved them up to Johnstown, where they would go on to star as the legendary Hanson Brothers in the classic movie "Slapshot." Actually, we called Jack up to join the Saints right before they were going to start shooting the movie, and Dave Hanson, a former Gopher from St. Paul, took his place. Well, the producers apparently liked his name better, so they wound up calling them the Hansons instead. What a great bunch of guys.

Only a couple of our guys had any significant prior NHL experience that first year, in Teddy Hampson, Mike McMahon and Wayne Connelly. Connelly was the best of the bunch and would lead the team in scoring with 40 goals and 30 assists. Hampson, meanwhile, would wind up serving as our longtime team captain. We were young, but that was OK. We had an exciting roster of players and as we soon found out, the fans were going to absolutely fall in love with us. Wow, what great fans we had in those days. That first year was a lot of fun. We played our first games in the St. Paul Auditorium, until the Civic Center was completed. In fact, our first game in the St. Paul Civic Center wasn't until January 1, 1973, in what turned out to be a 4-4 overtime tie with the Houston Aeros. In all, there would be 12 teams in two divisions: the New England Whalers, Cleveland Crusaders, New York Raiders, Quebec Nordiques, Ottawa Nationals and Philadelphia Blazers — all of the Eastern Division; as well as the Saints, Winnipeg Jets, Chicago Cougars, Houston Aeros, Edmonton Oilers and Los Angeles Sharks — all of the Western Division.

I remember the first game in the new arena was on October, 13, 1972. We wound up losing to Winnipeg, 4-3. The big story though was Bobby Hull, the league's biggest star. There had even been a big production prior to that in St. Paul when they presented Bobby with this giant cardboard check for a million bucks. The press just ate it up. You know, getting Bobby in the league at that time was quite a coup, it really was. The way it all played out was pretty interesting too. You see, all of the teams pitched in a hundred grand apiece, in order to pay him his whopping $1 million salary. He wound up in Winnipeg though because that particular owner put in more money and had a lot of pull with the other owners. Hull gave us instant credibility. He was probably the best player in the NHL at the time, and we stole him. Once it was announced that Bobby

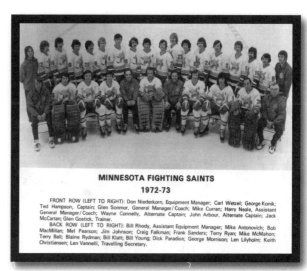

MINNESOTA FIGHTING SAINTS
1972-73

FRONT ROW (LEFT TO RIGHT): Don Niederkorn, Equipment Manager; Carl Wetzel; George Konik; Ted Hampson, Captain; Glen Sonmor, General Manager/Coach; Mike Curran; Harry Neale, Assistant General Manager/Coach; Wayne Connelly, Alternate Captain; John Arbour, Alternate Captain; Jack McCartan; Glen Gostick, Trainer.
BACK ROW (LEFT TO RIGHT): Bill Rhody, Assistant Equipment Manager; Mike Antonovich; Bob MacMillan; Mel Pearson; Jim Johnson; Craig Falkman; Frank Sanders; Terry Ryan; Mike McMahon; Terry Ball; Blaine Rydman; Bill Klatt; Bill Young; Dick Paradise; George Morrison; Len Lilyholm; Keith Christiansen; Len Vannelli, Travelling Secretary.

was jumping ship, it was a mass-exodus. The other players knew that if he left, then we were legit.

As for our franchise, we were pretty bare-boned when it came to running our operations, but we made do. There was no team plane or anything like that, we just scraped by and did what we could to make ends meet. It wasn't a very glamorous lifestyle, that was for sure. We wound up getting our first-ever win against the Chicago Cougars, when Mike Antonovich got the 3-2 game-winner late in the third. We had a pretty good team and we were tough as hell. There were a lot of fights in those days and the fans really loved that stuff. Gord Gallant wound up leading the league in penalty minutes. We set all sorts of league attendance marks that season, our fans were great. We finished the season with a pretty respectable 38-37-3 record, good for fifth place in the six-team division. We managed to squeeze into the playoffs but lost in the first round to Winnipeg, four games to one. All in all, it was a good year.

The following season I handed over the coaching reigns to Harry. It just got to be too much to coach and serve as the general manager, so I just focused on the latter. From there, we went out and got some colorful players in guys like Johnny McKenzie, Murray Heatley, Steve Cardwell and Mike Walton. Walton, or "Shaky" as he was affectionately known, was just fabulous and became a real fan favorite for us. He wound up leading the league in scoring that year, tallying 57 goals and 60 assists in 78 games. He was just an electrifying player. At one point during that season he went on a tear, scoring in a league record 16 straight games — including a stretch where he tallied 11 goals over three consecutive nights against Los Angeles, New England and Winnipeg. John Garrett was also added to the mix that year and both he and Curran played great for us in goal.

I remember one time that year when we were playing in Hartford. Harry had set up a curfew for the players and would check on them by calling their hotel rooms. Well, when he called Gord Gallant and Mike McMahon's room, Mike answered and told Harry that Gord wasn't there. Gord got in about an hour later after having been out at the bar. When he got in he called Harry to tell him that he was back, only the two of them got into a shouting match over the phone. Gord didn't like Harry because he always felt like he favored Shaky Walton over him and gave him preferential treatment. Harry just told him to sleep it off and that they would talk about it in the morning. Well, I guess that really pissed off Gord, who then proceeded to go out and grab a

Mike Antonovich

few more beers.

When he got back to his room this time he was really riled up. So, he called Harry again at about two in the morning and told him that he wanted to settle it right then and there. Harry told him to go to bed and hung up on him. A minute later Mike called Harry all frantic and said that Gord was on his way up to his room. So, he gets there and starts pounding on the door. Harry was rooming with Jack McCartan at the time, his assistant coach, and they both decided it would be better to just let him in and talk to him, rather than have him wake up the entire hotel. Harry then goes over to open the door and just as it opens, Gord jumps in and smacks him right in the nose. Harry went down like a ton of bricks. Jack then went at it with Gord after that and it got ugly. Harry, meanwhile, was out in the hallway and had nearly gotten knocked out cold. Jack finally got him out of the room, only to see him go after poor Harry yet again. Luckily he was able to fend him off though and shoo him away. We all met that next morning and made the decision to throw him off the team. He crossed the line on that one and even though he was a good player, we had to take a stand and get rid of him. That was one wild night, let me tell you.

The best thing that we had going for us as a team at that point was the fact that during the early 1970s the North Stars had gone into a terrible slide and were just playing awful hockey. We gained a lot of fans because of that. They were looking for something different and wanted to see some action. So, we tried to give it to them any way that we could. Whether it was guys scoring goals or guys beating the hell out of each other, we did what we could and tried to have fun doing it. The fans proved without a doubt that the Twin Cities could indeed support two pro hockey franchises. Even though neither of us were playing that great at the time, in reality it was a wonderful time for Minnesota hockey.

We played really well the following season, finishing with a 44-32-2 record, good for the second best record in the WHA. One of the highlights from that 1974 season occurred when Shaky Walton was named as the MVP of the WHA's All-Star Game, which was held at the Civic Center. What a night that was. Towards the end of the season I decided to add one more tough guy to our line-up for the home stretch. Edmonton had just signed this former football player who I guess was tough as hell and I wanted to make sure that we were going to be able to counter anything they might throw at us. So, I called my father-in-law down in Johnston and asked him who the toughest guy in the league

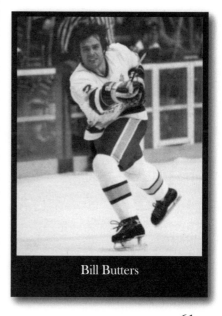

Bill Butters

61

was. He didn't even hesitate, he just said "That's easy, Goldy Goldthorpe." This kid was just an animal, having racked up a whopping 285 penalty minutes in just 55 games with the Syracuse Blazers of the NAHL. Well, I trusted Johnny's opinion. So, without any hesitation I immediately got a hold of him and signed him.

I remember going to pick him up at the airport. I was expecting to see a huge, six-foot-four, 230-pound gorilla step off the plane. Instead, I saw this little guy who couldn't have weighed more than 180 pounds soaking wet. I couldn't believe my eyes. It didn't take very long to see how mean and nasty this kid was though. God, he was tougher than hell. He would fight anybody. He had no fear whatsoever. I will never forget getting a phone call one night at about two in the morning from the night manager of the hotel where he was staying. He said that he had gotten into an argument with some gal and was scared to death that he was going to bust up the joint. So, I ran over there and got it all straightened out. Thank goodness he just slept if off, or it could have gotten really ugly in a hurry.

Now, we went on to beat Edmonton four games to one in the first round of the playoffs that year, and then faced the Houston Aeros in the second round. The Aeros were led by none other than the great Gordie Howe, who had come out of his two-year retirement that year to join his two teen-aged sons, Mark and Marty, to form the famed "Howe-Line." Gordie, now in his 40s, still managed to score 100 points that season. What a fantastic player he was. We played them tough, but they wound up beating us, four games to two, and that was that. The fans came out in droves though. We even sold out the Civic Center one night with more than 17,000 fans, which at the time was the largest crowd ever to watch a hockey game in Minnesota.

The one funny thing about that final series though, was how Goldthorpe just taunted old Gordie. He would scream and holler at him whenever he skated by our bench, threatening to tear his head off. I nearly lost it when he yelled out "Hey Howe, you can't play forever, and when you finally retire I am going to come after your two kids!" He was crazy, he really was. The fans here loved him. He would become infamous, of course, when his character "Ogie Ogelthorpe," was featured in the movie "Slapshot." The guy who played him in the movie, with that big bushy afro, was just a beauty. Whenever I watch it I just have to smile. They broke the mold when they made Goldy, he was something else.

Goldy Goldthorpe

We added some more guys that

next year, including former Gophers Gary Gambucci and Bill Butters. What a couple of great guys they are, I just think the world of both of them. In addition, we also brought up the guys from "Slapshot" fame, Jack, Jeff and Steve Carlson, as well as Dave Hanson — who had all been playing for our minor league affiliate in Johnstown, PA. They would truly put the "fighting" in Fighting Saints. Those guys were so much fun. We finished the 1974-75 campaign with a 42-33-3 record and went on to beat New England in the first round of the playoffs.

That was a rough series. In one of the games we set a total of eight WHA records for penalty minutes. There was a lot of bad blood there. The highlight came when Jack Carlson pounded on Whaler's tough guy Nick Fotiu, who was considered the undisputed champion of the league at the time. He had been a Golden Gloves boxing champion in New York early on and was really a feared guy. Jack just beat the crap out of him. It was brutal. He came back for round two later in the game and Jack flattened him again. Nobody could believe it. Jack had these huge knuckles and could really hurt guys. Man, he was tough. It was at that moment that Jack had gone from tough guy, to heavyweight champion.

A funny story about that happened after the game when the league, in an effort to save some money, booked both of our two teams on the same flight back to Minnesota for the next game. Well, I knew that this could get really ugly and potentially even dangerous if these guys got into round No. 3 at 30,000 feet. So, I told all of our guys to get on first and take the seats in the front of the plane. That way, when the Whalers got on they would have to walk past them and sit in the back, where we could keep our eyes on them. I will never forget seeing big Nicky walk down the aisle past us with these great big sunglasses on, to hide his fresh shiners that Jack had just given him. We made it back all right, but that was a tense flight, let me tell you. Anyway, the brawl swung the momentum for us and we went on to win the series. That is what a big fight can do to a team, it can get them fired up and bring them together. That is why Jack was just as valuable to me as was one of my top goal scorers. You see, without Jack out there protecting him, he wouldn't be able to score all of those goals.

From there, unfortunately, we wound up losing a seven-game heart-breaker to the Quebec Nordiques to end the season. Losing to Quebec was really tough. If we had beaten them then we would have played Houston in the next round, which, thanks to the Howe Line, would have guaranteed a couple of 17,000-

Here I am interviewing Len Lilyholm

63

seat sell-outs for us at the Civic Center. I will never forget how bummed out we all were after that game, especially Shaky Walton. You see, Walton was making about $150,000 grand a year at that time, which was by far the most on the team. He was a big tipper too, so the trainers used to really take care of him. They even let him park his big fancy Mark IV right inside the building, because he would always tip them so well. Anyhow, once we lost that game, he was so upset that he came off the ice and stormed right past the locker room and over to his car. He yells over to the trainer to get his wallet and keys for him out of the locker room and then just like that, he jumps in his car, in full uniform — skates and all, and just drives off. It was the craziest thing. That was Mike, he just did not want to deal with anything or anybody and decided that he wanted to get the hell out of there right then and there. He was a beauty, he really was.

We brought in some more new guys the next year, including Dave Keon, who I would have to say was the greatest hockey player that has ever played in Minnesota hockey history, at any level. He is a Hall of Famer and an absolute legend. He came to us out of spite I think. Harry knew him and got him to sign with us after he had gotten into a spat with the Toronto Maple Leafs over something or another. He was mad as hell with those guys for whatever the reason and simply refused to ever go back, so their loss was our gain. He was an odd duck, but what a great player. We also brought in a couple of local guys in Paul Holmgren and Henry Boucha, two of my all-time favorites. Paul was so tough too. He would later go on to coach in the NHL and is now the GM of the Philadelphia Flyers. What a great guy.

Things were looking good that season but eventually the bottom fell out from underneath us. You see, the team finally ran out of money and in February of 1976, after playing only 59 of 81 scheduled games, the ownership group was forced to file for bankruptcy and terminate us. We had a 30-25-4 record going up to that point in the season, and were really disappointed when the news was announced. It was tough, but that was just the way it went. We had seen it coming for a while. The team was losing money and the owners had been selling off our best players, which really hurt the team's morale. It was a fire-sale, just unbelievable.

The players had even gone like six weeks without getting pay checks at one point. We damn near had a mutiny on our hands after a while. The owners finally got a hold of some money and promised the players to pay them the equivalent of two games pay. I remember driving in a cab with Harry with this big envelope full of cash. We were both trying to figure out what each guy should be paid, based on 1/40th of his salary. It was crazy. We were literally living paycheck to paycheck at that point, not knowing if and when the team would fold.

It was at that point that I started to wonder if leaving the Gophers was the best decision after all. It was a particularly rough time. I wasn't sure what I was going to be doing with my life after that. I was stressed out, which only led to more problems. For the first time I realized that my drinking was now becoming a serious problem. I had gotten a reputation by this point and that was starting to effect me. I mean as soon as it was announced that we were out of business, Harry got a job right away with Hartford. Not me. I was having a tough time and it made me come to the realization that maybe my drinking was becoming a factor. I had a little bit of time off so I figured it would be a good idea for me to just take it easy for a while.

Just when I thought I could relax though, I found out that my father had died of lung cancer. Alcohol had finally gotten the better of him and I was so sad that he was never able to find his way out of that dark abyss. So, I went up to spend some time with my mother. I even helped run my father's pool hall for a while. I had also gotten divorced by this point, in 1975, as well. Margaret and I had been married for 22 years and it was just time, we both knew it. I had moved out a couple of times over the past several years and we both needed to move on. Our daughter, Katherine, was in college up at Duluth by this point and that made the decision to separate much easier for both of us. I then fell in love shortly thereafter with a gal by the name of Marcia. She had just gotten out of a marriage as well and we just connected. We would ultimately get married a couple of years later.

Eventually, I got a call from the owner of the Cleveland Crusader's franchise, Nick Mileti, to see if I was interested in taking over as the head coach and GM of their team, which was going to be relocating to Miami. I just fell in love with the whole idea of getting to coach down there in the middle of the winter. It was just what I needed at the time. I remember flying down there to meet with them in Fort Lauderdale and calling Harry from the beach one day while I was drinking a cold beer. I said "Harry, have a hell of a time up in New England this January you S.O.B., I am going to be down here in hockey heaven!" With that, I was officially the new head coach of the upstart Florida Breakers. Sadly, four days later the whole thing fell apart. Sure as hell, Harry couldn't wait to

The 1973-74 Fighting Saints

call me and rub it in by telling me how cold it was going to be in Minnesota that winter.

But, as luck would have it, Mileti, who also owned Cleveland's pro baseball and basketball teams, the Indians and Cavaliers, decided to move the Crusader's to Minnesota instead. He called me again and just like that I was back in business. We would return to the Civic Center and be renamed as the "New" Fighting Saints. They even replaced our old blue and gold sweaters with red, white, and gold ones — giving us a whole new look. Meanwhile, I went back to serving as both the coach and general manager again, and it was a lot of fun to be right back in the middle of the action. I was able to bring back some familiar faces too, in Dave Keon and Mike Antonovich. We also got Billy Butters, the Carlsons, Dave Hanson, Pat Westrum, Gord Gallant, Danny Gruen, Al McDonough, Ron Ward, John McKenzie and Lefty Curran. I was really excited.

We started out just great that year and were playing well. We had some tough dudes on that team and were really playing some physical hockey. Then, just like the year before, the bottom fell out from underneath us. In January of 1977, after having posted a respectable 19-18-5 record, the team announced that it was folding. We couldn't believe it. Everybody was designated as a free agent and just like that it was over. That ownership group was so cheap, it was tough. They didn't want to sign anybody to any long term contracts, which made it pretty tough to get guys in there. And, anybody who was any good got sold off for cash. It was a hell of an experience being around all of that, it really was. I was just sad to see it all end the way that it did.

Looking back, even though it all ended way too soon, I still have a lot of fond memories of those days. One of the funniest stories I remember from being with the Saints came early on up in Duluth, where we had an exhibition game one time.

Paul Holmgren

Well, the referee for the game that night was none other than Bill Friday. Friday was a very well respected and quite famous NHL referee who had jumped ship and come to the WHA. I had actually known him when I was a kid from Hamilton and he was a real good guy. He was a former player and pretty tough in his day. Anyway, I am up there introducing him around to everyone before the game. The reporters were all there too of course, including the beat-writer from the St. Paul paper, Don Riley. So, I introduced Bill to him and said "This is Don Riley, an outstanding writer from the Pioneer Press." Bill's eyes then got real big and he yells out "You're

Don Riley?! You no good sonofabitch, I have been looking for you!" He then pulls out his wallet and unfolds this old newspaper clipping that he has been carrying around with him for God knows how long. He holds it up and says "You're the guy who wrote this, and now you're finally going to get what's coming to you!"

Now, let me go back for a second and explain a little bit about Riley. I just love the guy. He was a little guy who just said it like it was. He didn't care if he pissed anybody off. His columns were notorious for the fact that he would just put whatever was on his mind in there. He was a beauty. If it interested him, he put it in. Well, it turned out that a couple of years earlier, Riley was upset over some bad call that he felt Friday had made which cost the North Stars a game. So, he wrote in his column this crazy theory on the reason why Friday never gave the North Stars any good calls was because some big blonde had turned away his advances at a bar one night and his payback was to screw the team out of any good calls. Of course it was all a bunch of B.S., but Friday didn't know that.

So Friday points to Riley and says "My wife saw this and she gave me hell over it. You just made this up you no good mother-f----er!" He wanted to make a big scene right then and there with poor Riley, and I had to jump in between them to make sure he didn't kill him. I said "Bill, calm down. I know Don and he was just goofing around, he didn't mean anything by it." Riley was scared as hell at this point, but I was able to talk to Bill and defuse the whole thing. Well, the funny part of the story happened later that night. Riley, who was a big drinker in those days just like I was, went and had about a half a dozen beers. The next thing I know, he comes over to me after getting all fueled up with some liquid courage and he says to me real seriously, "Glen, I've been thinking about this all night and I think I can take him." He says "Come on, I know that you know him pretty good, how should I go after him? Should I hook him to the body or should I try to nail him with an uppercut?" I just about crapped my pants at that point I was laughing so hard. I said "Don, for Christ's sake, you had better get the hell out of here before Bill sees what is going on. He might just be crazy enough to come over here and really let you have it!"

Luckily, I persuaded him to just go back and have another beer and to just leave it alone. Thankfully, that is what he did and that was the end of it. That was something else though, I will never forget that one. You know, Don finally got sober years later and I couldn't have been happier for him. He struggled with it for a lot of years like I had. He would hang out at Galivan's Restaurant in downtown St. Paul, that was his spot. Truth be told, he really inspired me and gave me hope to get sober too. I just love Don, what a great guy.

I got into a few fracas' over the years when I was coaching in the WHA, because the fans at those games were just wild. It was fun though. Nowadays you can get sued and arrested for that stuff. Back then they just let it go on and figured it was all a part of the show. The fans were a big part of our success and they were right on top of us in those smaller arenas. I remember one time during a game up in Winnipeg there was this really obnoxious woman who had been heckling me all night. So, I eventually turned around when there was a lull in the action and very loudly said to her, "Excuse me ma'am, how much do you charge to haunt a three-bedroom house?" The Jets fans in that section really got a kick out of that one and luckily for me, it finally shut her up.

Harry and I got into our fair share of skirmishes over the years too. But we always had each others backs, no matter what. That is how it is in hockey, you take care of your own out there. I remember one time when Harry was coaching and I was up in the broadcast booth doing the radio color commentary for the game. I saw out of the corner of my eye this guy run over to our bench and start climb up the Plexiglas. Once he got up there he dumped a full beer right on poor Harry's head. I mean he drenched him. He then jumped down and started to jog up into the stands. He was playing to the crowd and they were cheering for him as he hammed it up by taking a bow. I remember being on the air, live, and I said to my broadcast partner, Frank Buetell, "Please excuse me for a moment, there's something I have to take care of...". So, I took off my headset and went after the guy. By now he figured he was in the clear and was smiling and high-fiving the fans. So, I ran out from the press box and met him head on out in the stands. He looked right at me, like "who the hell are you?" and I just drilled him. I mean I really nailed the guy and he went tumbling backwards down the stairs. It was hilarious. I then calmly went back up to resume my broadcast duties like nothing had happened. Harry saw the whole thing and gave me a little wink to thank me.

Speaking of suits, I will never forget another time up in Ottawa when I was coaching with the Saints. There was this drunk fan who was really riding me hard the whole game. I remember I was wearing this really fancy blue velour jacket with some plaid pants, which I must have thought was in style back then. Well, I didn't care so much about this guy heckling me until he started calling me "Liberace." That was the last straw. So, in between periods I told Harry to go over and sit by the guy because after the game I was going to confront him. Sure enough, the game ends and I ran right up there to get a crack at this idiot. As soon as I got there I grabbed him by his tie and asked him if he had anything cute to say to me. He started to walk backwards in an attempt to escape, but there was Harry, who shoved him right back into me. I let him have it but good. It was great. Before long though some other fans joined in and it started to get out of hand. Just then the players realized what was going on, so a bunch of them raced over to help out Harry and I. Some of them were already half naked from getting undressed, but they came roaring up into the stands to rescue us from what quickly turned into a mob scene. Luckily we made it out alive after that one. Sometimes I miss those days in the old WHA. Those were some crazy times, they really were.

Ch. 7
Sweet Home Alabama...

I had a little bit of time off after the Saints folded, but was contacted shortly thereafter by the owners of the WHA franchise in Birmingham, the Bulls. They offered me the head coaching position for the 1978 season and I took it. It only wound up lasting for a year, but it was a pretty interesting experience coaching hockey in the deep south. I will never forget making my first impression to the owner when I missed the team flight to Quebec for our very first road trip of the year. I had been out drinking the night before and just flat out slept through my alarm. Well, I caught the next flight up there and made up some excuse as to what I had been doing. Then, when I got back, the owner sat me down and told me that he was fining me a thousand bucks. My reputation had preceded me and he knew what I had been up to. He basically put me on notice by telling me that if my drinking became a problem, then I was going to be fired. Well, I stayed clean for the rest of the season and as a result, the owner gave my the $1,000 back, which I really appreciated. That was a real wake up call for me, but apparently not enough to get me to quit drinking for good.

Living and coaching in Alabama was a real trip, let me tell you. They didn't play the National Anthem before our games down there, instead they played "Dixie" and they all waved their Confederate flags around. It was something else. It was football country. Alabama's legendary coach, Bear Bryant, was like a God down there at the time, and the only hockey that they were interested in seeing was the kind that was very similar to football. Translation, they wanted to see hitting and fighting, and a lot of it. Old Bear used to say with his thick southern accent "We're going to put the hurt on them...", and that was what we knew we had to do too in order to sell tickets down there. I knew right away that it was going to be a wild and crazy season.

We had some pretty good players on that team, guys like Frank Mahovolich, who was about 41 at the time, and Paul Henderson, the hero of the fabled 1972 Summit Series between Canada and Russia. We also had Tim Sheehy, from International Falls; Kenny Linesman, a phenom who was only about 18 at the time; Rod Langway, who would later win a

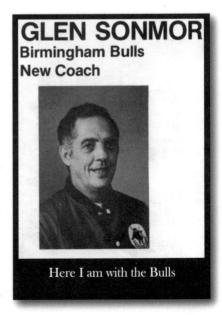

GLEN SONMOR
Birmingham Bulls
New Coach

Here I am with the Bulls

couple of Norris Trophies as the NHL's Most Valuable Defenseman; Mark Napier and goalie John Garrett. Defensemen Pat Westrum and Brent Hughes, along with center Joe Noris were also added from other franchises that had folded. It was a fun group of guys.

One of the stars of our team was a Czech kid by the name of Vaclav Nedomansky. What was interesting about him was the fact that we wound up trading him, along with Sheehy, to the Detroit Red Wings in what would become the first ever trade between the WHA and the NHL. In addition to a bunch of cash, in exchange for him we got Steve Durbano and my old buddy Dave "Killer" Hanson, of "Slapshot" fame, two of the toughest hombres in the game at the time. What is funny about that transaction, however, was that our owner, John Bassett, had a teenage daughter by the name of Carling, who would go on to become a very famous professional tennis player. It turned out that the deal almost didn't go through because Nedomansky, who had been a professional tennis player back in Czechoslovakia, was also her coach. So, Bassett didn't want to trade away his daughter's instructor that he was getting free lessons from. I just had to laugh over that one. Here the guy was saving nearly a million bucks over the life of Nedomansky and Sheehy's contracts, yet he was worried about losing free tennis lessons. Unbelievable.

Anyway, I knew exactly the type of players that they were looking for when that deal went down and could see the direction that the owner wanted to go. We were going to be tough and physical and that was fine by me, hell yes. The fans down there just ate that sh-- up. We had some serious red necks come out to our games and they wanted to see some fights. So, we gave it to them. The guy who was usually right in the middle of all of our fights was Steve Durbano. What a beauty that guy was. God, he was tough. He was a little bit crazy too, which always made for some interesting road trips.

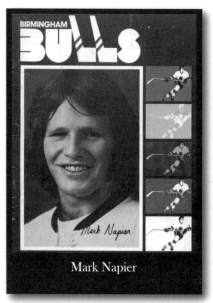

Mark Napier

I will never forget one time when we were out on the road in Cincinnati and at four in the morning getting a knock on my hotel room door. I answered it and it was Durbano, who was just beside himself. I said "Steve, what's the matter? Are you OK?" He then proceeds to tell me that he has to go home, back to Birmingham, right away. He explained to me that his wife, who was this bomb shell former go-go dancer, was really pissed off at him. She had apparently been looking for him and called his hotel room to try to get a hold of him. Well, we had him rooming with Frank Mahovolich, who was in his 40s at the time, and wasn't about to make up some B.S. story to cover for Steve. So, he told the truth and said that he was out dancing at a local bar. She went through the roof when she heard that. Apparently, they had some sort of stipulation in their marriage that said Steve was not allowed to go out dancing without her — a "no dance clause" if you will. You can't make this stuff up. Well, Steve called her when he got in and supposedly lied about where he was and then the sh-- really hit the fan. He said that she had thrown all of his clothes and everything he owned out the window and was just going crazy.

To make matters worse, he said that she was going to strangle his dog. Steve just looked at me all teary-eyed and said "Glen, I just love that dog...". I nearly lost it at that point. This guy was totally off his rocker, it was absolutely hilarious. I mean here is this guy, one of the toughest, most feared fighters in all of hockey, just weeping about his poor dog that was about to be murdered unless he could get home right away and save it. I just wished him luck and told him he could take a few days off to get things figured out. He was happy as hell after that and just took off for the airport. What a beauty that guy was. He was really something. You know, Durbano had been thrown off several other teams before coming to Birmingham for all the trouble he had gotten into over the years. Once he got here a sportswriter asked me how I was ever going to be able to control him. My response to him was simple. I said "What makes you think I want to?"

Durbano got into some trouble with the league later that season during a game against Quebec when he deliberately shot a puck at a referee. He got fined and suspended for that one, but he didn't care. He had been suspended plenty of times. He, like many fighters of that era, drank too much and that made him do things that he would later come to regret. You know, after hockey he moved up to Yellowknife, in Canada's Northwest Territory, and battled drugs and alcohol for years. He even wound up spending a considerable amount of time in prison. Sadly, he died in 2002 at just the age of 50. He was a lost soul, he really was. He was a good guy though and would do anything for his teammates, and that is why they loved him.

I will never forget the fracas that Durbano started later that year up in Winnipeg during the playoffs. Winnipeg's owner, Ben Hatskin, had a lot of clout with the league and he made sure that they had some referees in there who weren't going to allow us to intimidate them. They knew that our style was to be rough and tough and quite frankly, they didn't want anybody messing with the league's meal-ticket, Bobby Hull. So, we knew that we were going to have to try to play them straight up, only they were just too good. So, Durbano tried to stir up some sh-- with Bobby and went after him out on the ice. Sure enough, the referees tossed him out of the game, so he went and got showered up.

Well, they wound up beating us and we all headed into the showers a short while later. Durbano, meanwhile, is all dressed and ready by this point to get on the bus. So, he stepped outside to wait for us in this area below the stands by the rink. Well, a whole bunch of drunk fans saw him standing there and went down there after him. I just happened to step out of the locker room for some odd reason at that exact moment and saw what was going on. He was holding his own pretty good, but I could see a whole bunch of other fans about to jump in and really mess him up.

So, I immediately ran back into the dressing room and yelled out "Durbo's in trouble!" Everybody came racing out of there so damn fast, it was unbelievable. They just dropped what they were doing and took off. Our guys came flying out of there and all hell broke loose. In fact, Frankie Beaton didn't have time to put anything on, so he came running out buck naked. It was crazy, let me tell you. He didn't care. He just jumped in and started swinging. I remember him standing there after he took care of a couple of fans and screaming out "Are there any other heroes out there?!" He later said that the thing that made him the most upset during the entire melee was the fact that there was a cute broad who was staring and laughing at his little unit. He apparently wasn't very well endowed and was more offended by that than anything else. Plus, it was cold in there. Anyway, the whole thing was like a scene out of the wild-wild-west. Luckily the cops showed up to break it all up before things got really out of hand. I even got into the act too. I figured, hell, why not? It was fun.

We wound up getting hot towards the end of that season. Dave Gorman, Steve Alley and John Stewart caught fire and became known as the "GAS Line." The fans at it up. They led us into the post season, which was a first for the franchise, but we wound up getting beat by the Jets. We terrorized opposing teams through toughness and intimidation that year. It was a tactic and it worked. We even set a major league hockey record for penalty minutes, breaking the old mark which was established by Philadelphia's infamous "Broad Street Bullies," of the NHL. The Cincinnati newspaper even ran an editorial cartoon about us that year with the headline "Glen's Goons," and showed me leading four bloodied tough guys into a rink with chains. The four goons were Dave "Killer" Hanson, Frankie "Never" Beaton, Gilles "Bad News" Billodeau and Steve Durbano. People wondered why Durbano, the toughest of the bunch, didn't have a nickname — to which I would respond, "He didn't need one, all of the opposing players knew he was f---ing crazy."

All of our guys were characters and we all stood up for each other. Hockey down there was a tough sell and we had to find a way to fill up the seats in our arena. Say what you want, but the fans loved it. Hey, it's like the old saying goes: "If we don't stop all this fighting in hockey, we're going to have to build bigger rinks." Sure, some of the fans didn't care for our style of play, but that was what the management demanded. So, I did my job and gave them what they wanted. I tell you what, there was never a dull moment with those guys.

I will never forget the time Dave Hanson got into a fight with Bobby Hull up in Winnipeg. The two started going at it and somehow Bobby's toupee got ripped right off his head and wound up getting stuck in Dave's knuckles. It was one of the funniest things I had ever seen in my entire life. His rug then fell to the ice, at which point Bobby just scooped it up and raced off to the locker room. He then came back out onto the ice with a helmet on. It was unbelievable. It didn't even phase him though because he scored a goal just a few minutes later. Poor Dave didn't know what to do, he just kind of apologized to him and tried to play dumb. Luckily, Bobby was nice about it and let him off the hook. Otherwise all hell could have broken loose up there.

By now the league had been struggling financially. There were just eight teams left at this point, with the franchises being Houston, Indianapolis, Cincinnati, Hartford, Quebec, Winnipeg and Edmonton. They would ultimately last for two more seasons before folding. Before going away for good, however, four of the franchises were merged into the NHL: the Hartford Whalers (now the Carolina Hurricanes), Quebec Nordiques (now the Colorado Avalanche), Winnipeg Jets (now the Phoenix Coyotes), and the Edmonton Oilers — who were led by a young kid by the name of Wayne Gretzky.

Looking back, I think the league did wonders for the sport of hockey in general. Not only was it fantastic for the growth of American hockey, it also became a safe-haven for a lot of older players, as well as Europeans, who wanted to extend their careers. And, it was a showcase for countless younger players who wanted an opportunity to prove themselves. In the end, many of the kids who were given a chance as teenagers in the WHA, went on to become the stars of the NHL in the 1980s. The league wasn't afraid to try new things and provided a lot of entertainment for millions of fans throughout its nine year run. I was sad to see it go, it was a lot of fun.

"From Glen I learned that you can't have all great players on your team. He felt that you had to have a few tomahawkers, a few skilled guys, and a good blend of guys with grit and character. He always said though, that you need five or six brutes out there to protect your good guys, and intimidate the other team. Glen had a great vitality for life. When I played for the Stars, Lou Nanne never liked to play me, but Glen did. Lou said to Glen jokingly, 'You have to start looking at Butters with your good eye Glen, so you can see just how bad he really is!'

One time when I was playing with Jack Carlson for the Fighting Saints and we were losing to Hartford in the playoffs. Glen called us into the locker room to chew our butts. He said 'What the heck is going on out there? Look at you guys. Just look around the room. What do you think you're here for? Your good looks and hockey ability? Heck no! I want you guys to start a brawl out there, and I don't want it to end! We're going to win this series, and when that puck drops I want this place to go crazy!'

I wasn't a great player, but I knew that as long as Glen was in hockey I'd have a job because he knew that I'd play hard and physical for him." — *Bill Butters*

Ch. 8 Seeing Stars...

Towards the end of our season in Birmingham, I got a call out of the blue from my old friend, Louie Nanne, who wanted to know if I would be interested in coming back to Minnesota to work with the North Stars. Louie had recently retired from playing and had just been promoted to serve as the team's general manager. Ted Harris and Andre Beaulieu had both been behind the bench that year, but due to the team's poor play, Louie finished out the season as the team's head coach. Louie hated coaching, but was a team guy and wanted to do whatever he could to help the organization. So, he finished up the year and was getting ready to hire a new coach for the 1978-79 season.

Anyway, when he had gotten hired to be the GM, the owners had asked him who he thought he wanted to hire as his new coach. He told them that he wanted to hire me, to which they apparently said "now way." They didn't like the fact that I was coaching in the rival WHA at the time and were not interested in bringing me in. Louie stuck to his guns though and said that if they didn't like his choice, then they could find a new GM. Sure enough, they gave him the green light to bring me in.

Louie called me right away to tell me the good news. He told me that he had convinced them to look past the fact that I had coached in the WHA, but that they had other concerns about my drinking. Louie said "Glen, I personally don't think you have a drinking problem, but some of the people on the board think you might. So, would you mind flying in for an evaluation?" Now, I knew that I had a problem with it, but like most alcoholics, I was great at hiding it and even better at denying it. So, early that Summer I flew in and went to some outpatient counseling down at St. Mary's Hospital in Minneapolis. Luckily, they told me I was all right and that I wasn't that bad off at that stage. What a relief. I wanted that job so badly and would have done just about anything to get it.

Meanwhile, later that Summer I found out that there were big changes brewing over at the North Stars' front office. It turned out that the team had just merged with the cash-strapped Cleveland Barons. The nine Minnesota owners had wanted to get out, so they sold their interests to the Gund brothers, George and Gordon, who had been struggling ever since they had bought the California Golden Seals franchise a few years earlier and moved it to Ohio. Ultimately, when

Here I am with the Stars

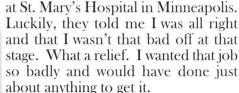

the merger was announced, the Cleveland franchise folded and all of the players who were under contract with the Barons became the property of the "new" Minnesota North Stars.

With that, the Gunds named Harry Howell, who had been the GM with Cleveland, to serve as the new coach of the Stars. As a result, I wound up working with the team's player development and scouting departments instead. I didn't really mind to tell you the truth though because I was just happy to be out of Birmingham and back in Minnesota working with an NHL franchise. Plus, I knew Harry from when were teammates together back in the early '50s with the New York Rangers and really like him.

So, I moved back to Minnesota and dove in head first into my new job. I was happy as hell, let me tell you. I even started going to some sobriety meetings again for my drinking problem. The counseling and the meetings worked for a while and I was clean for about six months. I was very busy and focused on my work too, which helped a lot. I took it pretty seriously because I wanted to keep my job. Before long though, I was sneaking drinks and falling back into my ways. You see, back in those days you would only go to meetings one day a week. I would go, but I would show up right before they started and then leave right when they got over. I didn't want to get involved with any of the people though and was just showing up because I had to. As I would learn, however, that doesn't work. Unless you are committed to getting sober and want to be there, then you will fail time and time again. That is the problem with alcoholics, we don't want to give up control. We think we can handle anything, but as we all eventually find out, we can't.

Then, as luck would have it, I wound up taking over as the team's head coach in November. It turned out that Harry was having some health problems and his doctors advised him to take it easy. So, he and I just swapped jobs, with him taking over as the director of player development. It was a dream come true to stand behind the bench of an NHL team, it really was. There were only 17 other men in the world at the time who had head coaching jobs at that level and I was very proud to say that I was one of them. I remember telling Louie how much I appreciated him going to bat for me. I just couldn't thank him enough for giving me that opportunity. It was just understood that I was going to be on notice with regards to my drinking, however, but I figured I had everything under control.

I would inherit a pretty decent team on the ice that year as well. With

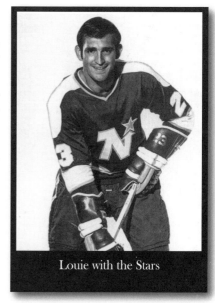

Louie with the Stars

75

the Cleveland merger we wound up getting some pretty good guys in here. The new team was allowed to protect 12 players from the original North Stars roster, including: Tim Young, Glen Sharpley, Per-Olov Brasar, Bryan Maxwell and Pete LoPresti; and then from Cleveland the team acquired: Gilles Meloche, Dennis Maruk, J.P. Parise, Al MacAdam, Rick Hampton, Mike Fidler and Greg Smith. All told, there were eight former Barons who made the North Star's opening day roster. Right winger Al MacAdam, who finished second in team scoring that season, and goaltender Gilles Meloche would prove to be the best of the bunch. We had a great nucleus of young talent on the team and I was really excited about our future prospects.

The star of our team though was rookie sensation Bobby Smith. Just getting him in Minnesota is a story in itself. You see, in those days the team with the worst record got to select first in the draft. There were no ping-pong ball lotteries like you see today. Well, everybody knew that the No. 1 player the year prior was Bobby. He was a phenom in the Junior ranks, where he had scored a whopping 194 points for the Ottawa 67s that season. Louie had told me a great story about how they got him. You see, with just a few weeks to go in the regular season, it was between the Stars and the Washington Capitals in a race to finish dead last. We were just one game worse than they were and Louie was determined to keep it that way.

So, he brought up all these kids from the minors to give them plenty of ice time. It was great. Their GM, Max McNab, would call Louie, who was coaching the team at the time, and ask him, "When the hell are you going to win another game?" to which Lou would say, "Just as soon as you do Max!" Sure enough, the team finished in the Norris Division cellar that year and wound up getting Bobby with that top pick. What a fantastic player he was. He went on to score 74 points that year for us and was named as the 1979 NHL Rookie of the Year.

Trying to stay fit...

We also drafted Smith's Ottawa line mate that year too, Steve Payne, who was a great player. We wound up putting Smith and Payne on a line with Al MacAdam and they tore it up for us. We ended up improving a great deal that 1979-80 season, finishing with 68 points in the standings, up 23 points from the year before. We missed the playoffs, but I knew that we were about to turn the corner. That next year we added a bunch of great guys like Craig Hartsburg, Curt Giles and Tommy McCarthy. Louie even signed Dino Ciccarelli at a time when everybody said he couldn't skate because of a rod that he had in his leg from a bad injury. But, Louie liked little Italians with a whole bunch of spunk and determination. I think they reminded him of himself.

You see, Dino had been a great player in Juniors, but teams were reluctant to sign him because he wasn't very big. Louie fell in love with him though when he had heard the story about how tough he was. You see, Dino had been playing with London, in the Ontario Junior Hockey League, and his big rival at the time was Al Secord, who played for Hamilton. Those two really hated each other. Secord was tougher than hell and most guys were scared to death of him. Not Dino, no way. In fact, one night when the two teams were playing against each other, Dino wound up scoring the game-winning goal. He was standing right next to Secord in front of the net when it happened and the picture of that exact moment was in the newspaper the next day. So, Dino, wanting to taunt Secord, cut it out and mailed it to him with a note saying "Where were

MINNESOTA NORTH ST★RS *Met Center, Bloomington, Minnesota 55420*

GORDON GUND, *Vice-Chairman of the Board*

December 1, 1978

Mr. Glen Sonmor
MET CENTER
Minnesota North Stars
7901 Cedar Avenue South
Bloomington, MN 55420

Dear Glen:

While we had a chance to congratulate you briefly during lunch at the Met Center a few weeks ago, I want to tell you again how pleased George and I are to have you as Coach of the North Stars. Along with Lou and the other members of the North Stars-Met Center Management Team, we believe your abilities, knowledge of the game, no-nonsense leadership and enthusiasm are just what is needed to shape a winning team out of our talented, but young and inexperienced, players. Your influence is already visible in the spirit of play of the team and will surely begin to be reflected soon in the record of the team.

Again, congratulations. You have our best wishes for the significant success that we are all confident you will achieve with this very challenging opportunity.

Sincerely,

Gordon Gund

Here is a letter I got from our team owner, Gordon Gund, that meant a lot to me. Gordon was one of the smartest hockey minds I have ever known.

you on this play, you big dumb-ass?"

When Louie found out about that, and about how big this kids balls were, he signed him immediately. Well, Dino would go on to play nearly 20 years in the NHL and score more than 600 goals. Louie was a great judge of talent and was right on the money with that one, that was for sure. Dino and Secord would go at it for years in the NHL and really made those North Stars vs. Chicago Blackhawk games a lot of fun. Our fans used to just love chanting "Secord-Sucks! Secord-Sucks!" And likewise, the Blackhawks fans would beat the crap out of those green "Dino the Dinosaur" inflatable toys at the Stadium in Chicago. It was a great rivalry we had with them in those days. Anyway, Dino got called up midway through the season and played very well for us.

Now, it is important to note that from April of 1973 to April of 1980, the North Stars had won a grand total of zero playoff games. The team had struggled and the fans had stayed away in droves. That was all about to change. I could really feel the momentum swinging our way at this point though, and knew that we were on the verge of not only making it to the post-season, but maybe even making a run at the Stanley Cup. We had some great players and I could just sense something good happening for us. Sure enough, the next season we went from the Adams Division basement to third place with a 36-28-16 record.

One of the highlights from that season came on January 7, 1980, at the Met Center, when we ended the Philadelphia Flyer's unbelievable undefeated streak which was at 35 games and counting at the time. Behind the chants of "Go Home Flyers," we beat them soundly, 7-1. That was a real feather in our cap to beat those guys. We got into some good brawls that night too, it was a lot of fun. It was such an emotional lift for us that it actually started our own streak, where we set a club record by playing 12 consecutive games without a loss at home. From there, we wound up cruising into the post-season, where we went out and swept the Toronto Maple Leafs in the opening round. The fans were just beside themselves. They had been so starved for a winning hockey team around here and I was so thrilled to be able to give that to them. Plus, to go back to Toronto as the head coach of an NHL team was really a thrill as well.

From there, we pulled off a major upset by beating the defending Stanley Cup champion Montreal Canadiens, who were attempting to go for their fifth straight title. The fans were just unbelievable that series. I honestly don't know if I have ever been in a building that was louder than the Met Center in those games, it was just deaf-

Louie was great with the media

ening. We won Games One and Two, lost Games Three, Four and Five, and then won Games Six and Seven. The finale came down to the wire, with our top scorer that year, Al MacAdam, notching the game-winning goal with just over a minute to go to put us ahead for good, 3-2. Gilles Meloche played great in goal and we really took it to them. I will never forget seeing all of the faces of the stunned Montreal crowd when we won that last game. It was something else. We were really on a roll, but it all came to an end shortly thereafter when the Flyers beat us in five games to win the conference semifinals and advance on to the Stanley Cup Finals. I think when we beat them earlier in the year to end their streak we might have rubbed it in a bit too much and given them just the incentive that they would need to kick the crap out of us. We were just emotionally spent I think and didn't have any gas left in the tank. It was a hell of a run though, it really was.

Shortly after that first season I wound up getting a big dose of reality when my drinking finally got the better of me. I had been sneaking around that year quite a bit. I must have thought that no one had seen me out running around, but apparently I was wrong. One day my daughter came and got me and told me that we had to meet Louie over at his office on a Saturday morning for some reason or another. When I opened the door I could see right away what was going on, it was an intervention. Louie was there, as were my assistant coaches, Murray Oliver and J.P. Parise, and our trainer, Doc Rose. My good friend from the University was also there, George Lyon, as was my wife.

Now, the basis for interventions is that the people who love you most are put into a room and they tell you that they are prepared to cut you out of their lives forever unless you seek immediate help. Clearly, my job was on the line too. Most people get very defensive about those things when they are sprung on them, but not me. I didn't fight it for a second, I was ready. It was a wonderful sense of relief to tell you the truth. I knew that I was in trouble at that point and I wanted help. I was flattered that they all thought so much of me to reach out to me, to tell you the truth. I didn't deserve it, that was for sure.

They wound up sending Marcia and I first to Florida, where we spent about 10 days just relaxing in the sun on a vacation. I never drank a drop down there, I just took some time to reflect and clear my head. Then, I flew out to this world renowned treatment facility called Care Manor, just outside of Los Angeles. I stayed for 30 days and learned a lot of things about the disease and

J.P. Parise

about myself. It was very enlightening being there, it really was. I did everything that they told me to do there, plus more. I really wanted to do everything I could to beat this damn thing. With that, I came home and got sober for what would turn out to be a little more than a year. I was scared straight and thought everything was going to be fine. I was going to meetings after that and thought that I had it under control. Eventually, after getting too confident in myself, I figured that I could handle a drink or two. Of course, I was dead wrong. It was just a matter of time after that before I started sneaking around again.

One of the things that helped me to stay sober that year was a relationship that I had made with a fellow patient out there by the name of Jim K.. He was a really sharp young guy. We would go to meetings every night together and really opened up to each other. He was suffering from both drugs and alcohol and was terrified to go back to his home, because he knew that he would fail back in that environment. Well, we were going to get discharged at about the same time and I could see that he was really in trouble. So, I invited him to come live with Marcia and I back in Hopkins for a while until he felt strong enough to go home. He was so grateful I can't even tell you. He lived in our basement for a few months and it was actually really good for both of us I think, to have each other as a support group. We would go to meetings together and it got him over the hump. He wound up moving out after a few months but stayed in Minnesota for about five years before moving back to California. He was just to afraid to be around his old friends in that toxic environment. My old buddy George Lyon hooked him up with a job at one of the big banks here in town and he wound up doing just great. He even met a gal from here and married her. Well, I am proud to say that he has been sober ever since. He is also a really successful businessman now and owns his own investment company. He couldn't be happier. I

My view from the bench...

feel so good about being a small part of that, I really do. What a wonderful story.

Anyway, I couldn't wait to get back on the ice when I got back from California. That is where I felt most at home, at the rink with the guys. We had had a great run the year before and were happy to make a run in the playoffs, but the bar had now been raised. The next season was going to be one to remember. In fact, I think a lot of people would agree that the 1980-81 team might just be the greatest in Stars history. We started out playing some solid hockey that year and just kept getting stronger as the year went on. There was one game towards the latter part of the season, however, that really had an impact on the psyche of this team. It was against Boston on February 26, on the road at the Garden. We had never beaten Boston in that arena, ever, in the history of our franchise. We were something like 0-27-7 over the past 14 seasons. They had absolutely owned us, it was ridiculous. The bad blood had started several years earlier when one of their tough guys, John Wensink, had skated over to our bench during a game one time and challenged every guy on the team to come out and fight him. Well, nobody budged.

Anyway, I was tired of those sonsofbitches intimidating us, so I decided that the "Curse of the Bruins" was going to come to an end right then and there. By that point I knew that we were going to wind up facing them in the first round of the playoffs that year and I really wanted to make a statement. I wanted to instill a new attitude of toughness into our guys and really encourage them not to take any sh-- from those a-- holes. That is so important in hockey, not to be intimidated or disrespected by your opponents. I remember just before the game a reporter asked our enforcer, Jack Carlson about the "Wensink incident." He asked him what would happen if something like that happened again. Jack just smiled and said "I would jump over the boards in a hurry and go after the guy because I would hate to have my coach beat me to him!"

As it turned out, we would wind up losing that game, 5-1, but I didn't care about the score at all. I wanted to send them a message that we weren't going to be pushed around anymore. So, I told our guys before the game that we had to make a stand right then and there. I told them that we were never going to beat them until we stood up for ourselves. I even held up a Boston newspaper that had an article in it about how the Bruins had dominated us and that we were basically a bunch of pussies. I told them that they were questioning our manhood. I really tried to get them riled up and mad as hell. My instructions to them in the locker room just prior to the opening face-off were simple. I told them that not on the second time, or the third time or even the fourth time, but on the first time that any Bruin tried to intimidate one of them, that they were to drop the gloves. I told them that we were going to war that night and that we were going to keep going to war until the game was over. Period.

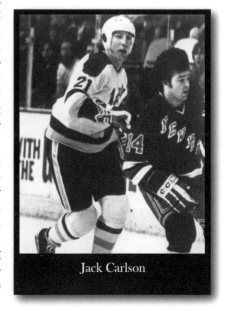

Jack Carlson

We had a lot of tough guys on our team. In addition to Jack Carlson, who was probably the toughest heavyweight in all of pro hockey at the time, we had Brad Maxwell, Dave Richter, Al MacAdam and Gordie Roberts. So, I felt pretty good about matching up with the "Big-Bad Bruins." It wasn't those guys who I was talking to about dropping the gloves though, it was everybody else. I wanted everybody to get into the action and really let their emotions out. I wanted them to experience just how good it felt to stand up for yourself and stop being bullied.

Well, sure as sh--, just seven seconds into the game our star player, Bobby Smith, who was anything but a fighter, dropped the gloves. Steve Kasper, one of their top agitators, had cracked him right under the chin with his stick during the opening face-off and that was just what the doctor ordered. As soon as Bobby dropped em', everybody else did too and we were off to the races. It was beautiful. That was how it was all night too. There was one fracas after another. I was never so proud to see at one point during the game, there were five fights going on and we were winning them all! I remember seeing Al MacAdam just beat the crap out of one of their toughest guys, Stan Jonathan. It was a blood bath. I mean there were over 340 penalty minutes in the first period alone, not to mention a total of 12 ejections. By the end of the game, there were 42 penalties, including seven game misconducts, and an NHL record 406 total penalty minutes. It just went on and on, it was really something. We only had about five guys apiece on the bench when it was over because so many guys had been thrown out of the game.

In the end we wound up losing the game, but I could have cared less. I was so proud of our guys, I could barely contain myself. Then, after the game I got into a shouting match on the bench with their coach, Gerry Cheevers. The next thing I knew my players were holding me back from trying to go after him. Hell, I wanted a piece of him. Sure, why not? I took a few swings at him from sort of an odd angle, where I was punching up towards him as he was leaning over the glass. Well, in the paper the next day there was a picture of me throwing a punch where my hand looked all goofy. I will never forget getting a phone call from my big brother shortly after that. Someone had sent him the photo and he couldn't wait to razz me about my girlish punching form. We both had a good chuckle over that one.

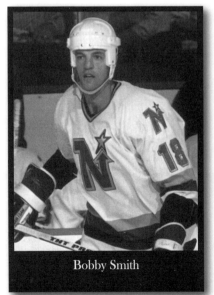
Bobby Smith

Anyway, down in the locker room after the game we were all pretty fired up. It was a scene straight out of a war movie, like we had all just returned from battle. It was great. The reporters couldn't wait to talk to me and get some quotes about what the hell I was up to. So, I am out talking to them and one of the reporters reads me a quote from Cheevers, who basically said that I was behind it all and that I had no character. I just smiled and said to the reporter and said, "OK, I have a message that you can take back to Gerry. Tell him to meet me between the dressing rooms the next time we play each other and we'll settle this like men. We'll see whose got character then." And then I added "Oh, and by the way, tell him to bring a basket to carry his f---ing head home in!"

I tell you what, we barely made it out of the Garden alive. Their fans came down and started rocking our bus, trying to bust the door down to have at us. It was scary, it really was. I thought we might have a riot on our hands, but luckily the cops showed up and escorted us out of there. It was a great flight home though. I remember looking at everybody with their fresh stitches, it was marvelous. We were victorious in my eyes because that just set the stage for our eventual meeting with them in the playoffs. It was just like that game against Omaha back in 1950 when I was playing with the Millers and John Mariucci led us to battle. The bad part of it all was that the league president called me into his office shortly thereafter and I caught hell from him. He asked me if I had incited my guys to play that way that night and I said "absolutely." I told him that we needed to make a stand and that I wasn't going to apologize for that. I got fined for it, but Louie gladly paid it for me. He knew what I was up to and was behind me 100%.

You know, when it comes to the topic of fighting, in addition to John Mariucci, I think I was influenced early on by Freddy Shero, who was a teammate of mine back in Cleveland. He was a quiet, unassuming kind of a guy, but he had a philosophy about the game where fighting was a legitimate strategy. Freddy, of course, would go on to become the architect of Philadelphia's legendary "Broad Street Bullies" during the early 1970s. He knew that his guys were collectively tougher than any other team in the league, so if his team was down he could send em' all out there to stir it up and really swing the momentum. It was a designed tactic to change the tempo of the game and it absolutely worked. They would just come in waves and beat the other team down until they didn't want to play. Hey, you can't argue with the results because they won a pair of Stanley Cups with that strategy. They won with fear and opposing players were truly scared of them. Sh--, once you can achieve that, the game is already half won.

I remember back then there was a joke in the league when players would get the "Philly Flu," just before they would have to play those guys because no one wanted to face them and get the crap kicked out of them. Nowadays you couldn't play that way. In fact, Freddy was the reason the league put in all of the rule changes that outlawed bench-clearing brawls as

Here I am giving em' hell...

well as the third-man-in rule. The rules have changed and really now you couldn't afford to have five guys in the penalty box, it would kill you. So, for me, I always enjoyed that kind of style and tried to use it to my advantage. And lets be honest, the fans loved it too.

You know, I have always told my players to be tough and to stand up for themselves. I never instructed them to go out and hurt anybody or anything like that, but I wanted them to protect each other out there. Guys like Jack Carlson knew their roles and didn't need to be told what to do. If they saw somebody take out one of our guys, then he just knew that it was his job to hold that guy accountable. That is how it works. I never punished a guy for not getting into a fight either, but I sure as hell wouldn't give him much ice time if he didn't feel it was that important to stick up for one of his teammates out there. The bottom line for me was that our guys had to stick up for each other, no matter what. If an opposing player tried to run our goalie, then he had to be dealt with right then and there, no matter what — even if that meant having to square off with a much bigger guy and getting punched a few times.

Fighting in hockey is a very controversial subject, but I am very passionate about it. While I don't believe it belongs in youth hockey, it has a place and serves a very important purpose at the professional level. There is a reason the pros don't wear face masks, because they have to be accountable for their actions out on the ice. If they play dirty or disrespect someone or take liberties with a smaller player, then they will have to pay the consequences for that. Hockey is such a beautiful game and one of the greatest things about it is the fact that it polices itself. The players handle their own issues out on the ice, like men, and resolve them. Sure, things can get out of hand from time to time, but there is an honor code in the game that has been around for more than 100 years. The players live by that code, it is what keeps the game honest.

Here I am signing autographs after a North Stars game

We learned the code as kids up in Canada. There were rules for how we conducted ourselves above and beyond the official rules of what the referees would enforce. It was a marvelous system based on honor and accountability. If you did something dishonorable or disrespectful towards another player, then you were going to have to answer to that by fighting. In fact, if you used your stick on a guy in those days, you were going to be taken to task not only by your opponents but by your own teammates. They too would make you stand up and take your medicine, otherwise they would be on the hook for your actions.

The code even went further than that though for the absolute superb players, who you almost couldn't even touch at all. You just didn't mess with the top guys in those days. That was a privilege that those elite few had earned. I remember one time when Pat Quinn absolutely leveled Bobby Orr on a beautiful open-ice check, nothing dirty about it at all, and then had to face the entire "Big Bad Bruins" team which came after him. Even Quinn's teammates were slow to come to his aid because when you nailed a guy like Orr, a superstar, then you had to be accountable for it. And of course when I was coaching the North Stars I also found it difficult to get my guys to even check Gretzky out there because they knew that as soon as they did they were going to have to turn around and face his bodyguards, Marty McSorley or Dave Semenko.

You know, when I was coaching the North Stars if another player was going to take liberties with Neal Broten or Dino Ciccarelli, our two star players, then I was going to send one of our tough guys over to do the same with the other team's star players. That kept it even. And our tough guys didn't need to be told when and where to go, they just knew, that was their job. In fact, sometimes as a coach the toughest thing about those situations wasn't sending a guy out to fight, it was holding him back. I mean if we were in a close game and couldn't afford to be a man down on a power-play, then we had to show restraint.

The code works those things out though and eventually players who play dirty will get what is coming to them. Old Gordie Howe used to have a list he would keep of all the guys who cheap-shotted him over the years. He would wait until the time was just right and then POW!, he would get them with that elbow of his when the refs weren't looking. He was such a tough, respected player, one of the best ever. Guys feared Gordie, they really did. What was so amazing about him was the fact that not only was he so tough, but he could score goals almost at will. You don't see guys like him anymore, he was a one of a kind.

In all actuality, a lot of fans really do enjoy that aspect of the game. The league is probably not that sure just how many fans they would actually lose if they got rid of it either. The fact of the matter is that they may lose a lot more fans than they think if they ever did outlaw fighting. And once they took it out there is no way in hell they could ever put it back in. So, I don't think they will ever eliminate it to tell you the truth. Yeah, I like fighting in hockey, hell, a lot of people like to see a good scrap every now and then. It is a part of the game. Sure, we can live without the bench-clearing brawls and the unnecessary stuff, absolutely.

But the emotional, in the heat of battle fights are important for the game I think. Look, this is a very physical game played by very tough, physical players. They need to let off some steam out there every now and then, and fighting is a good way of letting them do that.

As for the future of fighting in pro hockey, I think it is here to stay. The new rule changes which were put into place following the lock-out of 2004 have really helped to clean up the game. By taking out the red line and calling more of the obstruction penalties, the game has opened up with much more offense. There is still a need for fighting though and it definitely works. The bottom line with fighting is that it actually cleans up the game, but most people don't realize that. Without it, guys could high stick other players or cheap shot them with no fear of any retribution. Fighting promotes accountability. It also is what earns guys respect not only from their opponents, but from their teammates. One only needs to look at the Anaheim Ducks, who won the Stanley Cup in 2007 after leading the league in fighting majors. So, it is a tactic that worked 50 years ago and it is a tactic that works today.

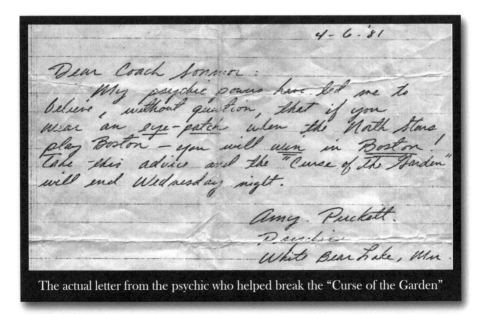

The actual letter from the psychic who helped break the "Curse of the Garden"

Ch. 9 The Quest for Lord Stanley's Cup...

Back on the ice, we finished up the 1980-81 regular season and went on to meet Boston in the first round of the playoffs. We usually didn't tinker with our roster too much at that time of the year, but we took a chance and called up a kid by the name of Neal Broten, who had just gotten back from winning a gold medal in Lake Placid as a member of Herbie Brooks' fabled "Miracle on Ice" Olympic team. Neal was from Roseau and had recently won the Hobey Baker Award with the Gophers the year before. He was just a fantastic prospect and we couldn't wait to get him out on the ice to see what he could do. We had even traded away centerman Glen Sharpley, which freed up Neal's lucky No. 7 jersey. Neal, of course, would go on to become the greatest player ever to wear the green and gold. What a great kid, just a hell of a player.

Now, just before we hit the ice at the Garden, I did something that I had never done before. I put on my eye patch, just like the old pirates used to wear. It is a crazy story of how I decided to put it on too. You see, just before I left for the airport from my house in Hopkins, I got a letter from a fan that somehow caught my attention. I was in a hurry, but for some odd reason I took a second to open it up and read it. It was from a woman in White Bear Lake who said that she was a psychic. She said that she had had a vision of me standing behind the bench in the Boston Garden with an eye patch on and that she saw us beating what she called the "Curse of the Garden." Her name was Amy Puckett, as in hockey puck, so I figured it had to be a good omen. Hell, I figured I could use all the good karma I could get at that point, so I ran back into the house and grabbed my eye patch. Anyhow, I put that patch on right before we hit the ice and I remember screaming out just like a general leading his troops to battle: "Boys, the curse ends tonight!"

We walked out onto the ice and the atmosphere in there was just electric. We had still never won out there up until that point, but thankfully that all ended in Game One when Steve Payne scored the game-winner at the 3:34 mark of overtime to give us a thrilling 5-4 victory. The curse had officially been lifted and we were on top of the world. We were expecting another blood bath, but they

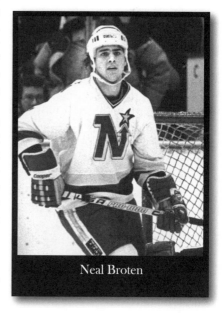

Neal Broten

played us straight up and it ended up to be a hell of a series. We then followed that up with a 9-6 victory in Game Two, behind our back-up goalie Donny Beaupre. From there, we came home to Bloomington for Game Three and it was just louder than hell in there. I mean the walls in the locker room were literally vibrating. It was insane. We were really confident in ourselves at that point and we went out there and finished them off by the final score of 6-3 to sweep the series. After the game legendary radio analyst Al Shaver said it was the biggest upset in Stars history. I would whole-heartedly agree, it was huge. More importantly, we had earned Boston's respect.

We had great camaraderie on that team and I had a fantastic captain in Paul Shmyr. He was such a good guy and so well respected by his teammates. He would take care of all of the little things that came up that I didn't need to concern myself with. For instance, he would handle all of the team fines if the guys were a few minutes late for practice or getting on the team bus, or even for staying out past curfew on road trips. He set up a system where all of the money went into a pot for a party at the end of the year. Paul would really get into it too. I mean he would have a trial for anybody who wanted to dispute their fines, complete with a big gray wig and robe, to look like an old English judge or something.

In fact, he had a name he went by "Judge Roy Beam." It was hilarious. He would hold court in the locker room with all of the other players serving as the jury while the accused pleaded his case. He would always turn to they guys afterward and either get a thumbs-up or thumbs-down from them. In all my years of coaching the Stars, I don't think I ever saw a guy get a thumbs-up, even if he was innocent. They wanted as much money as possible to go to the party fund to buy as much beer as possible, that was their main concern. I even got fined for taking the team to the wrong rink out in Vancouver for a practice one time. Then, after getting the proverbial thumbs-down, I wrote out a check for $25 bucks to "The honorable Judge Beam." We had fun with stuff like that, and that is what builds team chemistry — which is a crucial component for winning at this level.

You know, hockey is the ultimate team game and it takes a team of players, not individuals to win. That was very important to me. So, it was my job to get them to buy into that concept. As the coach I tried to make sure that everybody on my team had a role. It didn't matter if you were a goal scorer or a special teamer or a tough guy, I wanted everyone to have a role and to be the best at that role that they could be. I also wanted everyone on the team to realize that without all of the role players doing their jobs, then collectively we as a team would fail. I wanted our star players to really appreciate what guys like Mike Polich, Tim Younghans and Jack Carlson did out there, because without them doing some of the dirty work, we wouldn't score many goals. You just can't say enough about guys like Jack Carlson, he stood up for his teammates and always had their backs. If anybody wanted to take a run at Dino Ciccarelli, Bobby Smith or Neal Broten, and tried to intimidate them, then Jack would be right there to let them have it. Big Jack was the ultimate team player and that is why the fans loved him.

I loved hard working guys who didn't give a sh-- about all of the glory and recognition. I wasn't real high on big ego guys, they weren't going to last very long on my teams. And I didn't like complainers either who would run to Louie if they had a problem. Louie and I showed a united front from day one and wouldn't put up with any of that. So, those were a couple of the keys to my success early on I think. You had to be absolutely honest with your players about where they stood on the team. You couldn't con anybody, you just had to tell them where they stood, good or bad. Once you did that, then you could define specific roles for each player and make them feel important. I just tried to motivate each guy individually to do his best and work for the betterment of the team.

Sometimes I wanted Louie to trade away certain guys who I felt didn't fit into our system, but Louie would remind me that it was my job to get those guys to play better. He used to tease me that his wife could coach Broten and Hartsburg, and that it was up to me to figure out how in the hell to fire up the other guys. It was tough sometimes to coach guys who you knew didn't want to be there or weren't giving you their all. I was old school and didn't want guys around that were going to be a cancer for everybody else. If guys played hard for me and went to war with me, then I was going to be very loyal to them. If they were into themselves or into their statistics, then they weren't going to last very long in my system. I didn't care how good they were either, I just wanted the best players for our system, not necessarily the best overall players. There is a big difference.

I will never forget calling out Glen Sharpley in front of the entire team midway through that 1980-81 season and basically telling him that he wasn't pulling his weight and that his bad attitude was hurting the team. Glen was a guy who had scored 50 points for us four years in a row, so he was a good player. Sure enough, he ran right to Louie to tell him that it was me who was the problem, not him. Well, Louie could see what was going on and knew what he was up to. So, we shipped him off to Chicago shortly thereafter. It was a wake-up call to all of the guys though, about how important it was to stay positive and to put the team first.

Anyway, next up were the Adams Division champion Buffalo Sabres in round two. Steve Payne once again set the tone by scoring yet another overtime game-winner on the road for us in Game One. We cruised from there, winning both Games Two and Three, only to drop a Game Four double-overtime heart-

A rare moment of relaxation...

breaker by the score of 5-4. We rallied to take Game Five though and went on to win the series, four games to one. From there, we headed out to Calgary to take on the Flames in the conference semifinals. We made a statement in the series opener by crushing the Flames, 4-1. Calgary came back to win Game Two on a late third period goal, but we rallied back to take the next two games, 6-4 and 7-4. The Flames then won Game Five, 3-1, back in Calgary. We hung in there though and behind Brad Palmer's game-winner, we took Game Six, 5-3, and the series. With that, for the first time in franchise history, we had finally made it to the Stanley Cup Finals. For a Canadian kid who grew up dreaming of playing for a Stanley Cup, this was about as good as it could get. I mean here I was coaching a team that was four games away from winning it all. I could only imagine how good a cold beer might taste being chugged right out of the Cup after winning it all.

Well, the Finals were not going to be a walk through the park, that was for sure. In fact, it would be more like David vs. Goliath, with us being David and the defending Stanley Cup champion New York Islanders being Goliath. They were so good, a real dynasty in the making at that point. They had just swept their cross-town rivals, the Rangers, in the semifinals and were eager to hoist Stanley for the second time in as many years. We knew that we had our work cut out for us. They had the best defenseman in the league in Denis Potvin; the best all-around forward in Bryan Trottier; the best goal scorer in Mike Bossy; and the best playoff goalie in Billy Smith. They also had a very effective group of role players, penalty killers and big guys. They were a whale of a team because they had all the ingredients. They were just tough as hell and could score at will, what a lethal combination.

We opened the series out in Long Island. I thought our guys were prepared and looked good. They had their scruffy playoff beards in full bloom and were ready for what seemed like an insurmountable challenge. New York jumped out to a quick 1-0 lead on a goal by Anders Kallur though and never looked back. We made it interesting, but wound up losing the opener, 6-3. Dino Ciccarelli scored a power-play goal to give us a quick 1-0 lead in Game Two, but New York got goals from Bossy, Potvin and Bob Nystrom to make it 3-1. We rallied though and came back to tie it at three apiece in the second, on goals from Brad Palmer and Steve Payne. Just when we thought we were going to pull ahead, Potvin, Ken Morrow, and Bossy each scored in an eight-minute stretch to pull away for a 6-3 victory. Down two games to none,

Talking strategy...

we then headed back to the Twin Cities, where our fans couldn't wait to see us.

The Met Center parking lot was so full of tailgaters for Game Three that we could hardly even get to the rink. It was insane. They were all dressed up and so excited about how far we had come. It was a real Cinderella story, that team. The whole state was behind us, it was something else. Our guys fed off of that enthusiasm and jumped out to a 3-1 first period lead. The crowd was so into it, I could hardly hear myself think in there. We came out flying in the second period, but they rallied on a pair of Butch Goring goals to take a 4-3 lead heading into the third. We managed to tie it up at 4-4, only to see Goring get the go-ahead goal at the six-minute mark for the hat-trick. They added an empty-netter and came away with the 7-5 victory. We knew what to expect from their dominant guys, Potvin, Bossy, and Trottier, but I don't think we were prepared for so much offense out of Goring.

That was a tough loss, it really was. Our guys didn't roll over though, and we came out with a real sense of purpose for Game Four. I remember being in the locker room before the game and thinking of what I was going to say to the guys at that point. I wasn't much of a Vince Lombardi type of a motivational speaker, so I just wrote two words on the chalk board and left it at that: "NOT TONIGHT!" That was our slogan for the evening and it would serve us well. I will never forget the hit that Shmyr put on Potvin early in the game, just leveling him, that really set the tone. We got behind early in this one and thought that we tied it up at one apiece midway through the first period when Brad Maxwell scored on a slapshot from the blue line. We were all excited, but then we realized that the referee, Andy Van Hellemond, apparently never saw the shot and disallowed the goal. I just about went nuts. We later saw on the replay where the puck literally ripped right through the net and was in fact a goal.

There was nothing we could do about it because there was no video replay in those days. It got us going though and just a few seconds later Craig Hartsburg scored on a shot from the point that beat Billy Smith to tie it up. This time the red light went on and the crowd went crazy. Steve Payne then made it 2-1 midway through the third, and Bobby Smith added an insurance goal late in the game to give us the 4-2 victory. Our 19-year-old goaltender Donny Beaupre played just outstanding for us that night, he really did. It was a hard fought win and we were feeling pretty good about ourselves after that. We knew that it was going to be next to impossible to win out in Long Island, but the momentum was now on our side. Plus, I was just happy to give our fans something to cheer about. They had been with us all year and I really wanted that win for them more than anything.

From there, we headed back out to Long Island for Game Five. The Isles came out firing right away in this one and we didn't even really have a chance. Their line of John Tonelli, Bob Nystrom and Wayne Merrick was almost unstoppable. They scored 18 goals during the play-offs, all coming against the opposing team's top line. Goring, who was given the Conn Smythe Trophy as the playoff's MVP, added a pair of goals in this one and they went on to win the game, 5-1. With that, they had won the Cup. The win would be the second in what would be a string of four-straight Stanley Cup titles for one of the game's greatest ever dynasties. They had one hell of a team, just outstanding. I had to tip my hat to them. They beat us fair and square.

It was sad to see them all celebrating out there afterwards because I just wanted it so badly. Our guys were so down after that, we all were. You never know in this business if you will ever have a chance to get back to the Finals, and for me I never would. That would be as close as I would ever come to hoisting Stanley over my head. But we had a helluva team that year, and I was so proud of our players. I wouldn't trade that experience for anything. I've had a good many thrills in the game, but nothing to equal that. That was such a great team, with so many goal scorers and a handful of tough guys. We had some great players on that roster. Ciccarelli emerged as a star in the playoffs, scoring 14 goals and 21 points in 19 games, both NHL playoff records for a rookie. Bobby Smith once again had a big year for us in scoring 93 points, while Tim Young scored 66, Al MacAdam added 60, Steve Payne scored 58 and Tommy McCarthy chipped in with 48 of his own.

Tommy McCarthy was such a good player. You know, I will never forget what happened shortly after that final loss out in Long Island. Tommy was a good kid, but he drank too much. He reminded me of myself in many ways when I was that age. He was such a fantastic player, one of the best we have ever had here. Well, Tommy finally came to terms with his battle with alcohol when we had an intervention with him in Louie's office. I remember Bobby Smith telling him that he had more talent than anybody on the team, but that his drinking was holding him back. I wound up jumping on the plane with him to take him out to

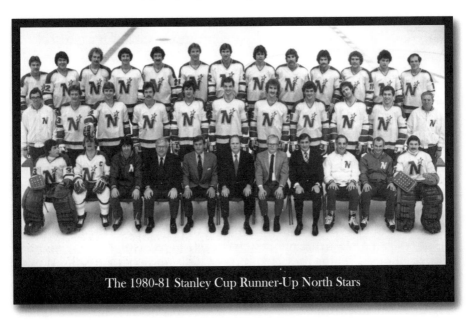

The 1980-81 Stanley Cup Runner-Up North Stars

the treatment center in Los Angeles that I had been at the year before. He really appreciated me being there for him, and I wanted to do whatever I could to help him out. He went through the program and then even came to live with us for a while at our house in Hopkins.

He was all right for a while but then got in trouble again that next year on a road trip out west. The players had a day off and decided to all go bowling. They figured that Tommy could have a few beers as long as they watched him and took care of him. What a huge mistake that was. Of course, they were dead wrong. That is not how this disease works. It turned out to be a big mess and that was really unfortunate. He struggled with it off and on for years after that. He played well for us over the next several years though, scoring at least 70 points in both 1983 and 1984. Had he gotten sober, however, and taken better care of himself, he could have been a perennial All-Star in this league. He later got into trouble for drug trafficking up in Canada and even spent some time in jail. That just broke my heart when I had heard that. He eventually got better though and is coaching in the Junior ranks up in Canada these days. I think of him often and hope that he is OK.

You know, I have worked with a lot of professional hockey players over the years in helping them beat this disease. One of those players was Link Gaetz, a former enforcer who played briefly with the North Stars. I was able to help him a great deal and we still talk over the phone about once a month. I would love to see him, but he can't get over the border right now due to some legal problems. Oh, his story is a sad one. As a player he was so good. He had so much talent and was so tough. He would be making $5 to $10 million a year right now had he been able to control himself. He just couldn't. That right there tells you what an awful disease this is. I remember recommending to Louie that we take a chance on him. We drafted him in 1988, the same year we selected Mike Modano. I will never forget when Louie sent me up to Canada to scout him and to spend some time with him. I knew that he was going to be trouble right from the get-go. I had never seen anybody who loved the stuff that money could get you as much as Link did. And I knew that he would like the difference between an NHL paycheck and a minor league pay check very, very much. I knew that really motivated him and that he was willing to do whatever it took to make it in the NHL. Ultimately, however, he was just never able to behave himself. It was a shame. He was so talented though, one of the best I had ever seen. I just hope that he can get his life in order now. In fact, he recently

Dino Ciccarelli

got some help up in Saskatchewan. My thoughts and prayers are with him as well.

The 1982-83 North Stars Front Office

Ch. 10 Finally Beating my Demons...

That next season we really played well. Expectations were running high for us and a lot of experts were picking us to go all the way. The fans were behind us like crazy too. You see, because of league expansion and re-alignment, we switched from the Adams Division to the Norris Division. With that came some great rivalries with Chicago, Detroit and St. Louis. That was such a good move for the league to do that, to align us geographically with those guys and build up those natural rivalries. Anyway, everything was going along great with the team. The only problem was that I had reverted back to my old ways and was drinking again.

I wound up getting into some trouble in mid-January of 1982 and ended up taking about a one week sabbatical from the team. My assistant coach, Murray Oliver, took over for me while I was gone. Truth be told, I had gotten caught driving drunk and wound up losing my license for what would turn out to be about two years. To tell you how bad it was, when the cop asked me where I thought I was at the time I got pulled over, I told him I was in Hopkins. Little did I know, however, that I had somehow wound up in White Bear Lake. Apparently I was lost and just driving around. I get so ashamed just thinking about that now. Thank God I didn't crash into someone and kill anybody. As a result, I had to take a lot of busses to get around and had to rely on others for rides to everywhere I wanted to go. Luckily, there was a very nice lady who worked for the North Stars at the time who would pick me up for work. It was humiliating, but I deserved it. Our fellowship says that if you get into a situation like that from your own stupidity, then you need to suffer the consequences. So, that is exactly what I did.

I got myself together after that and was able to lead the team back to the post-season. We finished with a club record 94 points, good for first place in the Norris Division with a 37-23-20 mark. Bobby Smith really emerged as a star in the league that year, scoring an amazing 114 points. Ciccarelli added 106 points on 55 goals and 51 assists, while Neal Broten added 98 points on 38 goals and 60 assists. Even though those guys played great that year, I still wound up bench-

Some words of wisdom...

ing Broten, MacAdam and Smith at one point during the season when each was in a scoring slump. I wanted to send a message to the rest of the team that even the top guys had to be accountable and needed to work hard every night. It worked too, because they would come right back after being a healthy scratch and the team would always win. It was an old tactic, but very effective.

From there, we wound up taking on Chicago in the first round of the playoffs. The series opened on April 7th at the Met Center in front of a packed house. We were seeded much higher than the Blackhawks and were expected to beat them without too many problems. Well, we wound up getting ahead of ourselves and sure enough, Chicago upset us. It was a big shocker. They won Game One in overtime and then took Game two, 5-3. We rallied to take Game Three in Chicago, where we just killed them, 7-1. We couldn't ride that momentum though and got beat the next night, 5-2, to end our season. Everybody was gearing up for another big playoff run, and we just played terribly. They had some good guys in Denny Savard, Doug Wilson and Al Secord, with Tony Esposito playing solid in net. Our power-play was just awful and we couldn't put the puck in the net. That was just the way it went. It was tough, it really was. I have to take responsibility for it though. It was my job to get the players ready to go and clearly I did not do that.

Before long there were rumblings in the press about how I should get canned because we had lost out in the first round. It is amazing how quickly they forget, I mean when I had gotten here just a few years earlier the team hadn't won a playoff game in more than seven years. Now they were ready to give me the axe because we got upset in the first round. Hey, that is just the reality of being an NHL coach. When things are going well you are on top of the world, and as soon as you hit a rough patch they want to bring in somebody else. The rumors were that either Herbie Brooks, Geno Gasparini or Dave King were going to be brought in. I tried not to pay any attention to it, but it was clearly a distraction. I started to get nervous though, because unlike a lot of coaches who deny it, I actually did read the newspapers.

I started to feel the pressure and naturally reverted back to what I knew best, drinking. That was my escape from reality. That was my friend who would always be there for me, no matter what. It is like a security blanket to so many of us, and for all the wrong reasons. Anyway, I worked hard that off-season on putting together a new game plan and it paid off. We lost just nine of our first 40 games and were really playing good hockey. Neal Broten was tearing it up, as was our newest rookie, Brian Bellows, who would finish with 65 points in 68 games that season. The entire line of Broten-McCarthy-Ciccarelli was even invited to play at the 1983 All-Star game, and they were also joined by Craig Hartsburg — who had taken over the role of team captain from Tim Young.

Everything was going great on the ice, but the press was still hounding me and looking for a reason to get me out of there. Louie assured me that I was just fine, but I made the decision for him to get rid of me pretty easy when I got into a helluva mess in Pittsburgh on January 12, 1983. I had been drinking a lot at this point and was starting to spiral out of control. We had shut-out the Penguins that night, 7-0, and I was feeling pretty good. So, I went out to a bar after the game to secretly have some drinks. Truth be told, I was going out to meet up with a gal who I had known from Pittsburgh. At the time my marriage with Marcia was failing and I was clearly not making very good decisions in my life. Well, she didn't show up and I got really upset. As a result, I hit the sauce pretty hard that night.

Eventually, when I was leaving to walk back to our hotel, two guys rolled me in an alley and beat the crap out of me. I don't even remember if I got in any good punches or if I was able to defend myself. It was just a blur. The police wanted me to press charges, but I was too ashamed and scared about the publicity that would surely follow. So I just got the hell out of there. I made it back to the hotel but was a real mess that next morning. I tried to disguise my black eyes and broken nose by wearing sun glasses on the plane, but people knew that something was up. Nobody wanted to come near me but I could tell that they were all whispering about me behind my back.

Afterward, I went in to see Louie and just told him "I need help." Right away he told me that he was going to make the arrangements for me to immediately go back into treatment at the facility that I had been at previously in California. It was a big relief. I wound up coaching the team that next night against Toronto, a 2-1 victory at the Met. Then, immediately following the game, we held a press conference for the media where I announced that I was going to be stepping down as the team's head coach to get some much needed rest from the stresses of coaching and that my assistant, Murray Oliver, would be taking over. I never actually said why I was leaving the team and where I was going though, because I was just too embarrassed. That was one of the toughest things I have ever had to do in my entire life. Everything I had ever worked towards was now gone, and I had only myself to blame.

Looking back, I can only wonder why in the hell I would knowingly put myself in a situation like that where I would ultimately wind up drunk in an alley with two muggers at four in the morning. Why we do the things we do when we are drinking is all a part of this terrible disease. I still can't figure it out. I mean here I was, one of just 18 coaches in the entire National Hockey League. Talk about an elite fraternity. I was making more than $100 grand a year, which was a lot of money in those days, and I was on top of the world. Then, I had it written right in my contract that if I was ever caught drinking again that I would be let go with no severance package, just flat out fired. They had every right to do that and I had agreed to it by signing the contract. They knew that I might be a liability, so they had that clause put in from the get-go.

Louie wanted me to go to treatment immediately but I was somehow able to convince him to let me go up to see my mom in Toronto for a couple of days first. As soon as he agreed to that I thought about just running away, I really did. I even went to the bank and took out a whole bunch of money just in case I was crazy enough to actually do it. I was a real mess. So, I flew up there and wound up camping out in this little hole-in-the-wall motel just outside of Toronto for two days. I couldn't even tell you the name of it all these years later. I sat in there and drank and drank and drank.

My wife didn't know where I was at that point, nobody did. Eventually, after two days of soul searching in this little dark room, I remember finally just getting down on my knees and saying "God, please help me." It was like a peaceful calm then came over me at that point. I can't explain it, but for me it was my moment of truth. That was my rock bottom. I'm not a religious person, but I know, absolutely, that I was saved by God's grace. There was no other explanation for what happened that night.

From there, I went back to the airport to fly out to the treatment center in California. Ironically, the flight had a lay-over back in Minneapolis. So, when I got there I called my mother to tell her that I was all right and that I loved her. I never even saw her when I was up there, I didn't have the courage. Next, I called my poor wife and told her that I was OK and that I was going back to the treatment center to try to get my life in order once and for all. Then, and I will never forget this for as long as I live, I got back on my flight to Los Angeles and immediately ordered two bloody mary's. I sat there in my seat staring out the window and calmly drank them as I thought about the mess my life had become. I then said to the stewardess as she came over to take the empty glasses away that those were the last two drinks I was ever going to have in my life. And do you know what? They were. That was January 17th, 1983, and I haven't touched a drop of alcohol since. I was 53 years old at the time and that moment was truly the new beginning for the rest of my life.

With that, I went to the treatment center with a new sense of purpose and was finally ready this time to get serious about beating this damn thing. I completely surrendered to the disease at that point and was able to get the help that I so desperately needed. I will never forget nearing the completion of my 30-day treatment program. Louie had called me and told me that he was going to be reassigning me to work in player development. I was fine with that, I really was. I was just thrilled that he had stuck with me and that I still had a job with the organization. He then told me that my first assignment would entail me heading up to western Canada to scout some tournament up there. The only catch was that it would have required me to leave the program one day early. I figured it would be fine because I had done so well and was

Brian Bellows

completely committed to staying sober this time around.

So, I went to my doctor to ask him if that would be all right. He just looked at me and laughed. He said "Glen, Glen, Glen, you still don't get it, do you?" He talked to me about accountability and responsibility. He reminded me that the most important thing in an alcoholic's life is that every single day he or she doesn't have a drink. Anything that he or she puts ahead of their sobriety, whether that is their job or family or whatever, they will ultimately lose when they start drinking again and succumb to the disease. I just nodded and apologized to the doctor for being so foolish. With that, I called Louie and told him that I was sorry but that I couldn't leave early. Louie was completely understanding and it all worked out. But that was a very eye opening experience for me about my new priorities in life. I have never forgotten that conversation to this very day.

Back in Minnesota, I returned to the North Stars, where, over the next couple of years, I would remain with the team and continue as a coach, assistant general manager, scout and director of player development. Basically, I did whatever I could to help the team. Louie had stuck by me and I was going to stick by him to help him in any way possible. As for the team, we wound up losing to Chicago for the second year in a row that season under Murray Oliver. Louie then wound up hiring long-time Canadian college coach Bill Mahoney to take over behind the bench for 1983-84.

Louie wanted to stir things up, so just 10 games into the season he pulled off a blockbuster deal that sent Bobby Smith to the Montreal Canadiens for Keith Acton and Mark Napier. In retrospect, I feel really badly about that because I know that it was partially my fault as to why Bobby left. He and I were close and when I left he had a hard time getting along with Mahoney. I think that Mahoney had tried to make an example out of him and was particularly tough on him in order to ingratiate himself to the other players. Bobby finally said to hell with it and asked to be traded. Bobby was one of the franchise's greatest players, so I was sad to see that happen. But, it was a business decision that Louie made and they did get good value for him in return. Incidentally, Bobby would later return to the team in 1990-91 and help lead them back to the Stanley Cup Finals that season.

The team played great hockey that year and once again won the Norris Division crown by posting a 39-31-10 regular season record. Broten, Bellows, Maxwell and Ciccarelli all played big that season, and the team went on to make a nice run in the playoffs. They got past Chicago in round one, then beat St. Louis in round two, but wound up getting swept by the Edmonton Oilers in the conference finals to end the season. I will never forget Steve Payne's overtime game-winner in Game Seven to beat the Blues in the semifinals, 4-3, that was something else. They just got killed by the Oilers in the finals though, losing four straight to a much better team. Led by Gretzky, Coffey, Messier, Linesman, Fuhr and Kurri, they would go on to win their first of four Stanley Cups in five years that season. They, like the Islanders of the early '80s, were the next great dynasty. What a team.

The team then opened the 1984-85 season with a miserable 3-8-2 record. Something had to be done, so Louie fired Mahoney and replaced him with yours truly. I will never forget the day that he brought me into his office and told me that he was offering me my old job back. I had been sober for about two and a half years at that point and couldn't believe my ears. That was such a proud moment for me because it told me that the organization had faith and confidence in me again. There was a lot of stress in coming back to coach again though, and some people were worried that the pressure might even get me to fall off the wagon. But I knew that I had changed my life around by then and would never go back down that road again.

It was wonderful to be back behind the bench. To be able to teach and coach at that level is so rewarding. Well, as a team we had our share of ups and downs that season, and we ultimately finished up the regular season 18 games under .500, with a 25-43-12 record. Despite our poor record, we were still able to sneak into the post-season, where we wound up scoring an upset sweep over the first-place Blues in the opening round of playoffs. Keith Acton was unbelievable in that series, scoring the game-winners for both of the first two games in St. Louis. Gilles Meloche then played outstanding in net for us in Game Three, notching a 2-0 shut-out to send us into round two. Next up were the Blackhawks and we managed to outscore them in Game One, 8-5. They took Games Two, Three and Four, but we rallied to win Game Five behind Dennis Maruk's overtime game-winner. We battled like hell in Game Six, but came up on the losing end of a 6-5 overtime heart-breaker. That was a tough game, it really was.

Louie brought in Lorne Henning to take over as the team's head coach the following season. I went back to the front office, where I focused on player development and scouting. I was happy. It was fun to have an impact on the team from another perspective. I was just glad that I was able to stay clean and sober. I had been worried about being one of the guys and about going out after games on road trips. I was stronger than I thought though and was able to change my habits and adapt just fine. I remember even going over to Germany one time on a scouting trip and winding up right in the middle of Oktoberfest. There were giant steins of beer being passed around everywhere, but I hung in there and just drank pop. I got some funny looks, but I didn't care. Anyway, the team played well that year and wound up finishing

Herbie Brooks

second in the Norris with a 38-33-9 record. They went cold in the post-season though, ultimately losing to St. Louis in the first round of the play-offs, three games to two.

The next year would be a tough one. The team struggled early and never played up to its potential. So, towards the end of the season Louie fired Henning and put me back behind the bench for the last few games of the season. The reason he got fired was because he went behind Louie's back, which really pissed him off. Louie had been out of town scouting somewhere and apparently Henning had brought in a couple minor league kids who he really liked without telling him. Louie got upset and canned him. It wasn't the best of circumstances for me to take over as the coach, but I was thrilled to be back behind the bench again. I knew it was a short term thing but wanted to show Louie that I was loyal and would do whatever it took to help the team.

I was just so appreciative to have an opportunity like that again at that stage of the game. We wound up finishing the season with a 30-40-10 record and missed the playoffs for the first time in eight years. It was rough. Little did I know but that was the last time I would ever coach again. When it was all said and done, I would finish as the team's all-time winningest coach with a 174-161-81 overall record, while also going 36-21 in the playoffs. I was proud of that and figured that nobody could ever take that away from me.

You know, losing my job and then getting it back years later was very special to me. That entire experience was life changing and really something that I am proud of accomplishing. I saw the importance of friends and learned to really appreciate those who will stand by you when you are down. Then, if you are willing to do the right thing, I saw first hand that you can come back and live out your dreams while learning some very valuable life lessons along the way. I was just blessed to have people who stood by me, especially my other guardian angel, Louie Nanne. Thank God for Louie Nanne, he stuck with me and helped me get through my darkest hours. He saw his friend falling apart and he helped me. He had to remove me from coaching, but promised to keep me in the organization if I would get help. I wasn't going to let him down again.

The next season we were able to bring in Herbie Brooks to serve as our new head coach. He and Louie were good friends and had played together on the 1968 U.S. Olympic team. Herbie had been up in St. Cloud State that past year, turning their program from Division III to Di-

Herbie & Louie as 1968 Olympians

101

vision I. He came there following his stint with the New York Rangers, where he had won 100 games quicker than anybody in team history. He came to St. Cloud because his former coach and mentor, John Mariucci, had told him to do so. John felt strongly that we needed more opportunities for more Minnesota kids, and knew that Herbie could get it done. The popularity of hockey in the U.S. was at its all time high following the "Miracle on Ice," and he knew that we needed to take advantage of that momentum. Herbie was a tireless promoter of the game and always did his part. So, he lobbied the state legislature to get St. Cloud's program a beautiful new arena and got them elevated to D-I status. It was just marvelous.

Well, it took some convincing, but we were able to get Herbie to take the job as the North Stars' head coach. It was something else to be able to finally work with Louie and Herbie at the same time, what a treat. Herbie was reluctant to take the job at first, but could never shy away from a good challenge. And speaking of a good challenge, that was exactly what he was going to get as the head coach of the Stars that year. The team played awful that next season due in large part to the fact that everybody was injured. The team actually set an NHL record for the most man-hours lost during a single season, it was that bad. And it was all of our top guys who were out too, Ciccarelli, Broten, Hartsburg, Mandich and Sargent, among others.

Everybody was on the shelf that year and in the end it turned out to be a total disaster as the team finished in the Norris Division cellar with a dismal 19-48-13 record. Then, towards the end of the season, Louie stepped down as the GM and took over as the team president. He had had a health scare that year and his doctor told him that he needed to step away from the stresses of the day to day grind. So, the Gunds let him run the team as the president, which allowed him to relax a little bit without all of the travel and what not.

Herbie was truly a one of a kind...

Meanwhile, Herbie now wanted to assume the role of both the coach and general manager, but the Gunds didn't go for it. Herbie figured that the timing was right for a long-term deal and knew that the Gunds were in a tight spot. It was a power-play, a real gamble, but he figured that he had them by the balls. The Gunds had a whole bunch of "f--- you money" though and got pissed with Herbie when he gave them what they took to be an ultimatum. So, they brought in Jack Ferreira to take over as the new general manager instead. As much as I loved Herbie, I had to agree with the owners on that one, and I told Herbie that. I felt pretty strongly that the team should have a separate coach and GM, otherwise it can cause all sorts of problems with the players. As a result, Herbie got upset and left the team. It was too bad because he was such a fantastic coach and really never got a chance to showcase his talents that one year with all of those injuries.

You know, losing Herbie back in 2003 in that tragic car accident was such a loss for hockey. What a guy. Herbie just had that special quality about him which made him a winner. He was so intelligent too. He had an ability to see everything that was going on around him and then was able pick out what was really important. Combine that with his unbelievable work ethic, and you knew he was going to be successful in whatever he did in life. As a coach, he was such a great tactician. His players maybe didn't love him, but they respected him and went to war for him. He was a no nonsense kind of a guy behind the bench and that was all part of what made him a success. He didn't let anything slide either. I mean if something or somebody had to be confronted, then he would confront that situation right away and get it behind him. And what a great motivator he was. He could get his players to do things that they never imagined they were capable of doing and that was just a marvelous quality. His honesty and forthrightness might have been his best qualities though. There was never any question as to where you stood with him.

Herbie set such an example for all of us with his absolute concern for the game of hockey. He truly championed American hockey, and even more specifically, Minnesota hockey. His commitment to making sure that Minnesota kids had every advantage was incredible, and we should all be grateful to him for that. He really carried that forward from John Mariucci's vision and that will probably be his legacy I think. So, all of us need to work a little harder to keep that going now that Herbie is gone. His commitment to make sure that Minnesota kids had every

The pall bearers at Herbie's funeral, what a tough day that was...

103

chance to succeed is what drove him. He would go to war over his beliefs and that is what made him so unique. In fact, I have not met anybody in my life who was more committed to what he believed in than Herb Brooks. And, he was willing to risk anything and everything to champion that cause. He just didn't care. He took up unpopular causes and wasn't afraid to stand up and say that something wasn't right. To me, Herbie was the result of giving of yourself completely to whatever cause you believed in and seeing it through to the end. Dedication and hard work just exemplified everything he believed in and I admired that in him so much. What a remarkable person he was.

Meanwhile, Ferreira went out and hired Pierre Page to serve as the team's next coach in 1988-89. Ferreira then basically let everybody go in the scouting department immediately following the draft that year, by handing them all an envelope with their walking papers inside. Real classy. Well, I stayed on but it was tough to work with Jack. He didn't want me around and wound up sending me all over the place to scout players that I had no business being around. I told him that for him to ask me to scout Junior games up in Canada, with all of my knowledge and experience, was like swatting flies with a sledgehammer. He just wanted me out of his hair. I wound up staying with the organization for the rest of that season before finally deciding to move on. The writing was on the wall for me. It was too bad, really, because Louie drafted Mike Modano that year and I knew that the team was on the verge of getting really good again. Sure enough, that next year the team made it all the way back to the Stanley Cup Finals, where they lost out to Mario Lemieux and the Pittsburgh Penguins. I am sad that I wasn't around for it, because it was a hell of a team.

Eventually, the Gunds were awarded an expansion franchise out in San Jose and wound up moving the entire front office out to California to make way for a new ownership group here in Minnesota. I had no interest in moving and knew that the new ownership group would be bringing in their own people. So I left on my own terms. I am proud of the fact that I have never been fired in my entire life. That means a lot to me too. It was a tough time for me but I got through it.

On a personal note, I also got divorced at about this time from Marcia. We had been together for 15 years, but it just wasn't working out. I had moved out and then back in a couple of times by then and it was just getting to be too tough. She had been through a lot with me over the years and I will be the first to admit that I was no picnic. All of the drama with the drinking and the rehabs and the sobriety eventually took its toll. So we both decided to go our separate ways. I was doing great with my sobriety though and was really able to lean on my new friends at the fellowship that I was so involved with at that point of my life. They were a real pillar of strength for me as I went through all of that. So, I wound up moving into a little place in Bloomington around that time, where I have been living ever since.

Ch. 11 New Challenges and New Adventures...

After leaving the North Stars I wound up going to work as a scout with the Philadelphia Flyers under Bobby Clarke from 1990 to 1992. I was able to remain living in Minnesota though, which was great. It was a lot of traveling, but I really enjoyed working with a new organization. It was a fresh start. From there, I went to work for a scouting combine group that was run by Marshall Johnson, a longtime NHL general manager. It was a sort of central scouting agency, which pooled its resources for several NHL teams. It too was a lot of fun and allowed me to stay involved in the game. I stayed with them for two years and then got a unique opportunity in 1994 to join the upstart Minnesota Moose, an International Hockey League expansion team that was setting up shop at the Civic Center in St. Paul.

You see, by now the North Stars had left town and moved to Dallas. They had been purchased by Norm Green, a real estate developer who was just a real piece of crap. He got into a bunch of trouble shortly after taking over the team when it was alleged that he had been sexually harassing one of his employees. Well, he didn't want to stick around and face the music, so he moved the team down to Dallas instead. What a sad day that was, it still breaks my heart. Like everybody, I was just devastated. I will never forget when they blew up the building a few years later, what a sight that was. I remember standing there with Louie when they pushed the button to implode it and it wouldn't fall down. Everybody started to cheer, it was something else. The old gal just didn't want

Blowing up the Met Center, what a sad sight that was...

Stephane Morin

to go down without a fight. That was a great place to watch a game with such good sight-lines, why they tore it down to make a parking lot I will never know. There were a lot of good memories in there, that was for sure.

Anyway, the team left in 1993 and the following year an IHL team was brought in to fill the void left by the Stars. The owners, Kevin MacLean and Roger Sturgeon, asked me if I wanted to serve as the team's general manager, or director of player development as they called it. I thought it would be a fun new challenge, so I agreed. They had hired Coleraine native Frank Serratore to serve as the team's head coach, with Mike Antonovich serving as his assistant. Once I found out my buddy Anton was going to be there, I couldn't wait to jump on board. It was an enjoyable time for me to be with a new team and to watch them grow as an organization. We played our home games at the Civic Center, as well as at the Target Center on occasion, and competed in the IHL's Western Conference along with Atlanta, Houston, Kansas City and Milwaukee.

We had some good kids too. In fact, Stephane Morin led the entire league in scoring that first year, which was really exciting. We wound up getting a lot of local guys on the roster too, like Reed Larson, Dave Snuggerud, Dave Christian, Larry Olimb, John Young, Kris Miller,

Here I am behind the bench with the Moose

John Brill, Brett Strot, Scotty Bell, Mark Osiecki, Tod Hartje, Chris Imes and Gordie Roberts, among others. The fans here really got behind us and quickly bought up all of the Moose paraphernalia they could get their hands on. I guess we even led all of minor league hockey in merchandise sales. We played all right that first year and finished the season with a 34-35-12 record, good for fourth in the division. From there, we made it to the playoffs but were swept by the eventual Turner Cup champions, the Denver Grizzlies.

That next season the team signed a working agreement with the NHL's Winnipeg Jets to become their minor league affiliate. And, after finishing the 1995-96 season in last place with a 30-45-7 record, Winnipeg soon became the team's permanent address. You see, the thing that ultimately killed the franchise was the fact that there were a lot of rumors at that time about how the Jets were going to be moving to Minneapolis and playing at the Target Center, with the Moose then in turn moving up there to take their place. Well, with all of these rumors going on, the poor guys who sold season tickets and did corporate sales were just having an awful time. Sure enough though, following the season the team moved up there, where they were renamed as the Manitoba Moose. The only problem though was that instead of the Jets coming here, like we all thought was going to happen, they ended up relocating to Phoenix instead, where they were renamed as the Coyotes. So, that was really sad too, to see them leave like that.

I even wound up coaching a few games there at the end with them too, which was a lot of fun to once again be behind the bench coaching a professional team. That last year I got to do all sorts of things with them, including some radio broadcasting with Greg Harrington for our road games. In fact, that would turn out to be a great break for me to be able to get my feet wet in broadcasting. I liked it and it turned out I was pretty good at it.

After the Moose left town I actually wound up going to work for the Coyotes. You see, Bobby Smith had recently been named as the team's general manager and wanted me to join his staff. I was thrilled. I again spent a lot of time on the road, but was able to continue living in Minnesota. I wound up spending about two years working with the Coyotes and had a lot of fun working that organization. In the meantime, I had also gotten hired in 1997 to work as a radio color analyst for Gopher hockey games. I just loved doing that, let me tell you. What a thrill it was for me to be back with the Gophers. My first broadcast partner was former North Stars an-

Greg Harrington and I in the booth

107

Al Shaver

nouncer Al Shaver. What a legend. Being on the air with him, as my first gig in the business, was like being put on a line with Gretzky as an 18-year-old rookie. You know, Al and I both grew up outside of Toronto as kids listening to the great Foster Hewitt, who did "Hockey Night in Canada" broadcasts. So, for us to be together at that stage of life was something else. We used to laugh like hell together up in the booth, reciting Foster's classic opening line: "Hello Canada and hockey fans in the United States and New Foundland, and a special big hello to Canadian troops everywhere..." What a voice that guy had, just amazing. Al and I just worshiped him as kids.

Anyway, Al and I did games together for a couple of years and then Dan Terhaar took over for him when he moved up to Vancouver. Dan and I had a ball traveling on the road together and telling stories for the next three seasons. He later left to work at WCCO radio and now does a fantastic job as the play-by-play announcer with the Minnesota Wild. When he left I was then joined in the booth by Wally Shaver, who I have really had a tremendous time working with over the past several years. Like his father, Al, he is just an unbelievable person and a real professional. Being on the radio with Wally is such a treat. He is one of my favorite people in the whole world. What a fantastic play-by-play an-

Wally Shaver

nouncer he is, maybe the best in all of college hockey. Wally is just a great person and a great friend. He is so pleasant to be around and we genuinely have fun together. It is a real honor to say that I have worked with both the Shaver boys, that is for sure. I also got a chance to work with both Eric Gislason and Rob Leer over the years too, who were both fantastic journalists as well.

In between all of that, in 1999 I joined Minnesota's newest NHL franchise, the Wild, as a member of the team's scouting department. There, I focus primarily on the college and high-school kids from the area and really feel good about being able to stay involved and contribute at this level.

Both jobs go hand in hand because I am constantly watching the top college kids with the Gophers, and then spend much of my other time scouting high school, Junior and elite league games. When the Wild came to town it was such a blessing. To see how that organization conducts itself is nothing short of incredible. Both jobs are fantastic, they really are. I mean to be gainfully employed at the age of 78 working with both the Gophers and the Wild is something I only could have dreamed of years ago. I am truly blessed to be doing what I love to do at this stage of the game.

As for my time with the Gophers as their radio color analyst, it has been absolutely wonderful. I don't take myself too seriously as a member of the media or anything, but I do feel that I do a pretty good job. People tell me that they enjoy listening to me, so that is probably the best indicator that I am doing all right. The greatest compliment we get is when people say to us that we sound like we are having fun. That is what it is all about. It is a real labor of love and my enthusiasm for this program and for these kids is genuine. You know, as a fan of hockey I certainly like listening to broadcasters who are enjoying what they are doing and have a passion for their jobs. So, hopefully for me when people lis-

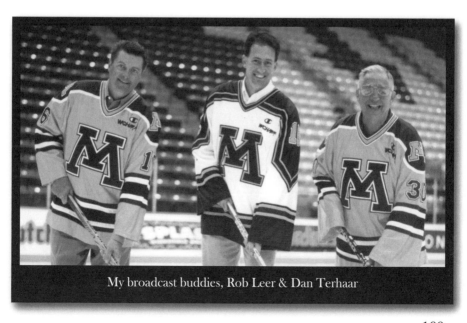

My broadcast buddies, Rob Leer & Dan Terhaar

Paul Martin

ten to me doing Gopher games they feel the same way. I love Gopher hockey so much and would argue with anybody and everybody out there that I am indeed the school's No. 1 fan.

You know, one of my jobs as an announcer is to pick the three stars after every game. They are usually all Gophers and I make no apologies for that. I remember a funny story that Al Shaver told me one time about Rocket Richard, the former Montreal Canadiens Hall of Famer who went on to do their radio broadcasts. He said that after a game one night between his Canadiens and the Red Wings, he picked the three stars. Al described the story using Rocket's thick French-Canadian accent. He said it went something like this: "For the first star I gotta take that Jean Beliveau, he gets two goals and one assist. For the second star, I have to take my brother, Henri because he don't get any points, but he played good defense and was all over the ice out there tonight. And for the third star, I guess I have to take that Gordie Howe from Detroit because, if he don't get those four goals, they don't beat us 4-3..."

I just feel so fortunate to be able to be a part of such a high caliber program. The team is a legitimate threat to win the national championship every single season and somehow manages to produce an abundance of outstanding student-athletes, year in and year out. There

Mike Crowley

is so much excitement in that beautiful arena each and every night we play there. What more could you ask for? I just love to watch the kids come in all bright eyed as freshmen and then watch them grow and develop into not only better hockey players, but into men. That is so neat to see.

As for my favorite players? Certainly Mike Antonovich was my favorite player when I was coaching. But now, as a radio broadcaster, I would have to say my favorite kid would be Paul Martin. What a class act. I wished like hell the Wild would have drafted him, but it just wasn't in the cards that year. He is such a great player though, and is on the verge of becoming an NHL All Star I think.

He is that good, he really is. Another kid who I really liked a lot is Johnny Pohl, who is now skating with the Toronto Maple Leafs. What a fantastic high school and college player he was. I just loved him when he was with the Gophers, what a classy kid. He is going to have a good career in the NHL too, because he is a really hard worker who has a great hockey sense.

Certainly another one of my favorites would be Mike Crowley. He was such a tremendous skater. I remember watching him when he was a star at Bloomington Jefferson and was just tearing it up. I would tell the other scouts about him and about how he was going to be something else. He was just a superb all-around player, one of the most electrifying I have ever seen. To me, he was more impressive than any other high school kid I had ever seen, including the likes of Henry Boucha, Bobby Krieger and Dave Spehar. I was scouting with Philadelphia at the time and practically begged them to take him. He was small at the time but I was con-

Watching the Gophers win it all in 2002 was such a thrill...

"Glen has been able to enjoy a wonderful life in hockey. More importantly, he has made a lot of friends along the way. Everywhere I go people stop me and tell me to make sure I say hello to Glen. I don't know anybody who doesn't like Glen Sonmor — even the guys he used to beat up! Really though, he is such a great person and so down to earth. There is a lot of respect for him in the hockey community. In our business we all aspire to be and do what he has done. He truly enjoys the game and has such a passion for life. He has been through a lot in his life but has come through it all with such dignity and respect. I have never met a man who loves the game of hockey more than Glen Sonmor. I can tell you that as the general manager of the Minnesota Wild, we are extremely lucky to have him on our scouting staff. He works the local high school, junior and college beat and is the best in the business at what he does. He is still one of the brightest hockey minds in the game today and we are privileged to have him working for us, rather than one of our competitors. And, aside from his hockey knowledge, the impact that he has on our staff is immeasurable. He has been such an outstanding influence on our staff and had such an impact on our organization in ways that he will never know. Glen has so much respect for the game and as such, I have so much respect for him." — Doug Risebrough

Thomas Vanek

vinced he was going to grow. The other scouts teased me about him non-stop because I was always talking about him. They just figured I was a homer rooting for my Minnesota kids, but I knew better. I knew that he was going to be really good.

Well, they eventually drafted him but traded him away shortly thereafter to Anaheim. He was playing well but the Ducks never really gave him a chance. I was eventually able to convince the Wild to acquire him when I started scouting for them. I remember watching him so intently during the pre-camp trials and he was looking very good. They were quite impressed with him and were going to give him a real shot to make the team. Then, sadly, during the last scrimmage, he wound up rupturing his Achilles tendon. A guy skated over it and it severed it right in two. I just felt awful for him. He got it fixed and tried to come back, but he had lost his greatest asset, his explosive burst of speed that he was known for. It ultimately cost him his career. I was sick about it. What a shame. I could relate, with my eye injury, so I knew how devastated he must have been. What a great kid though, I really enjoyed watching him.

There have been so many great players who have come out of here in the last 10 or 15 years. Guys like Jordan Leopold have been so much fun to watch. I think Keith Ballard is another one who is going to

Johnny Pohl

be a star at the next level. Gretzky just raves about him down in Phoenix right now with the Coyotes and says that he thinks he might have a shot at being their captain before long. What a statement from the game's greatest ever. Thomas Vanek is another one who is already an NHL superstar. I mean that kid just signed a $50 million contract, what a player he has become. They were so worried about him when he left the Gophers after two years, that he wasn't a very good two-way player, and he then goes out and puts up the best plus/minus mark in the entire league. That is amazing. What a gifted goal scorer he is, just something else. As of lately, I am really impressed with Erik Johnson and Kyle

"Working with Glen Sonmor is the biggest perk of my job, by far. To listen to Glen tell stories is one of my favorite things to do in the world. One of my favorite stories about my time with Glen happened one time up at Michigan Tech. We were there doing a series and just before we were about to head over to the rink for the game, I get a call in my hotel room. Well, it was Glen and he says 'Wally, I lost my eye...' Now, for those who don't know this, Glen lost an eye many years ago while playing in a hockey game, so he wears a glass eye. I asked him where he put it but he couldn't remember. He said he looked all over the room and couldn't find it anywhere. So, I went down to his room and we spent at least a half an hour on our hands and knees just scouring this hotel room for his eye. By now we had to get going or we were going to be late for the game. Glen says, 'No problem, we'll just head over to the drug store on the way over and I will pick up a pirate patch.'

The last time Glen lost his eye and had to wear the patch, all hell broke loose up in Boston in one of the greatest brawl-fests of all-time when he was coaching the North Stars. Great, now I am thinking it could get real ugly if somebody makes fun of his patch and he goes after them! Well, luckily, just then he found it — it was hiding on the bed spread. Apparently it had popped out and he lost track of it. Anyway, all was well and we headed off to the game. That eye has been around, let me tell ya! He even lost it on the bench one time during the National Anthem when he was coaching the Stars. The lights were off at the time and all the players were feeling around for it, it was a classic. Glen is the best. He makes my job so much fun, I just love the guy." — Wally Shaver

Okposo, who are both going to be stars in the NHL. They are so much fun to watch, I just feel privileged to be able to see them develop on a daily basis.

I would have to say the highlight of my time with the program as an announcer would be winning that first national championship back in 2002. That was so great to be a part of, just wonderful. I was broadcasting the game up in the booth and I can honestly say that I lost all journalistic objectivity as soon as Grant Potulny scored that game-winning goal. At that moment I was not a broadcaster, I was a Gopher. Hey, I am a homer and damn proud of it! I have been doing Gopher hockey broadcasts for a long time now and could see the frustration building within the program for so long.

So, when they finally did it, it was just incredible. And to do it in such dramatic fashion, winning it in St. Paul, that was just marvelous. To see the absolute joy of those kids out on the ice after the game was what it was all about. That is why we play this game and to see that raw emotion out there afterwards was very special. Don Lucia is really a fantastic coach. He commands a lot of respect and does a great job over there. I

"Traveling with Glen made for terrific stories every week. We were out in Colorado Springs one time doing a Gopher-CC series. Well, after a game one night Glen told me to swing by his room that next morning and pick him up for breakfast. So, that next morning I knocked on Glen's door to go to breakfast. I hear some shuffling around in the room and finally after several knocks on the door he lets me in. He is standing there in his tightie-whities and his room looked like a tornado had just gone through it. Stuff was everywhere. I asked him if he was all right. He said, 'My eye fell out in the middle of the night and I couldn't find the damn thing! Well, I finally found it over there behind the curtain.' I just about died laughing. He said it so matter of factly, and that was that. He said he would throw on some clothes and be with me in a minute. Sure enough, he popped his eye back in and we went and had breakfast.

You know, I learned so much from working with Glen, the guy is just a brilliant hockey mind. I mean he is much older than I am and only has one eye, but he could see things out on the ice that I would never pick up on. I was just amazed at the things he could see and how much he understood the nuances of the game. I love Glen, he is just the best." – Dan Terhaar

thought back to how close they had come in years past, under Doug Woog, and was so happy for everybody associated with the team. You know, it really had an impact on all of the Gopher alumni too, they all got to share in those victories as well.

Again, at this stage of my life I can't even really express just how happy it makes me to still be connected to Gopher athletics. I get so excited when the season starts and I can go down to watch the kids practice. I love to meet them and get to know them too. I take such pride in their successes both on and off the ice. I feel like a grandfather to all of those kids, I really do. They become such a big part of my life every year. I am like a little kid during the season, knowing that we have a big weekend series coming up against Wisconsin or North Dakota. I can't get to sleep before those series' because I am so nervous. I feel so blessed and appreciative to be able to do what I do. To see those kids and their raw enthusiasm for this great game, it just doesn't get any better than that.

Now, as for my scouting career

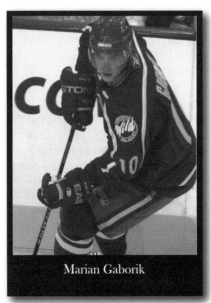
Marian Gaborik

with the Wild, what an honor it is to be affiliated with such a first class organization. These guys have done everything right from day one around here. They have built their team according to a plan that Jacques Lemaire and Doug Risebrough established from the get-go and they have stuck to it. Look at all of their high draft picks, nearly every one of them has panned out. How about that first draft back in 1999-2000, when they took Marian Gaborik and Nick Schultz, with their top two picks. Neither of them has spent a day in the minors and both are not only great players, but outstanding citizens. Jacques' teams play tough defense and they are disciplined.

Pierre Marc Bouchard

Plus, he is a proven winner and the players respect him. Hell, between he and Risebrough, they must have about two handfuls of Stanley Cup rings. They are both well respected in the hockey world and I feel very honored to be able to work with them.

They develop their players, they don't rush them, and they are committed to getting guys who fit into their system. They want players who can come in and be team guys first too, and will not be a cancer in the locker room. That is important to them, to acquire good character people. Look at this young crop right now in Koivu, Burns and Bouchard, who have all made a big leap as of late. This team is on the verge of doing some great things, it really is. Just wait. They have a great balance of goal scorers and defenders. Plus, they've got Derek Boogaard, who is probably the toughest guy in the NHL right now. If anybody messes with Rolston or Gaborik, they are going to have to face that guy — and that is not a very appealing proposition for most of their opponents.

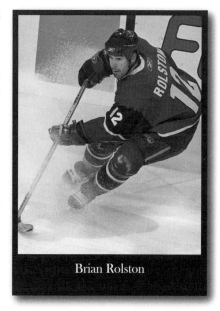

Brian Rolston

The fans just love this team too, which is so important in the overall success of a franchise. They have sold out every single game that they have ever played in over at that beautiful new arena, the Xcel Center, and there is a waiting list a mile long for season tickets on top of that. Again, I just can't say enough good things

Derek Boogaard

about this organization. Their marketing people, their sales people, the ticket-takers, everybody who if affiliated with that team is just top notch. They get it, they really do. I have been around a lot of hockey teams in my career and I can honestly say that this is by far and away the best, from the top down. There are not many teams in the National Hockey League that can even come close. It is only a matter of time before they are raising banners in the X, mark my words on that one.

You know, all in all I would have to say that the state of the state of hockey in Minnesota is fantastic. I think it is as good as its ever been and it only keeps getting better. We have so many dedicated youth coaches and volunteers working with our youngsters and that is what it is all about. At the prep level I think that the elite high school league, which has been going on for the past several years, has really opened the door for a lot of our top kids in particular. It has doubled the number of games these kids get to play and that is a really big deal. Minnesota kids can't make it with just 25 high school games a year. So, they need to get additional ice time in order to compete with the older, more experienced kids. This essentially is what the Canadians and Russians have been doing for years. They get the best players playing against the best players. This league has outstanding coaches and is really making a difference though. I mean they have had a bunch of high school kids selected in the first round of the NHL draft the past few years, which is just fantastic. All of the top kids are in this league and that is just going to enhance Minnesota's stock well into the future.

The college game is thriving here too. More and more kids are advancing on to the next levels, both boys and girls, and that is just great to see. With five Division One schools here, there are countless opportunities for Minnesota kids. I mean we have more than 200 boys and 100 girls every year getting D-I scholarships now, which is just remarkable. When I was coaching here back in the '60s that would have been inconceivable.

Darby Hendrickson

Then, with the Wild now firmly entrenched into the community, we truly are the "State of Hockey." What a place this is. Hockey fans in Minnesota are among the very best in the world, they truly are. Outside of a few places up in Canada like Toronto, Vancouver and Montreal, this might just be the hockey capital of the world.

Take a kid like Darby Hendrickson, who played in the high school tournament, with the Gophers, on the U.S. Olympic team and then with the Wild. Wow, what a dream come true. And he did it with such class. He represents the best of the best from our state and the benchmark for others to follow. I have seen a lot over the years and it has been

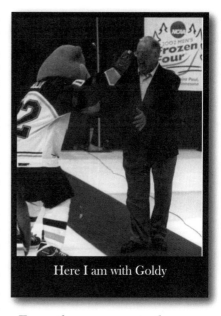

Here I am with Goldy

great to see just how far we have come. From the peewees to the pros, we just have it all here and I am thrilled to be right in the middle of it all.

What a crew: Doug Woog, Mariucci & Louie in front, with Brad Buetow, Herbie and yours truly in the back.

Ch. 12 My Guardian Angel: John Mariucci...

As I reflect back on my life, I can't help but think that it is really a story about guardian angels. Sure, I have been blessed to know some truly legendary people from the hockey world over the years, but none of them had a greater impact on my life than John Mariucci. I honestly believe that a higher power put us together nearly six decades ago for a reason. When I came to Minnesota to play with the Minneapolis Millers back in 1949, I was just a 20 year old kid with my whole life in front of me. John became like a second father to me and took me under his wing. I was in awe of him then and still am to this day.

Then, when I lost my eye several years later, he was there for me and made sure everything was going to be all right. He brought me here and practically adopted me. He convinced me to get my college degree and he got me into coaching. He gave me the tools to succeed in life and for that I will forever be grateful. I wound up graduating from the University with distinction, which is something I am very proud of. John had gone to all that work to get me in and I wasn't going to let him down. What a guy he was. I will never forget when they renamed the hockey half of Williams Arena after him. That might have been his proudest moment. He had bought a new camel hair sport coat for the dedication ceremony and got all dressed up for the big day. He was so happy. He later went down to get some ice cream at the concession stand and when they told him how much it cost he said, "The hell if I'm paying for this, this is my damn arena now!"

His legacy comes in the form of tens of thousands of kids who lace up their skates every Winter and play the greatest game on earth. His tireless work to grow the game not only Minnesota kids, but for American kids, truly changed the landscape of hockey in this country and inspired countless people to take up the game as either a player, coach or volunteer. We should all be so grateful for that.

When he died back in 1987 of cancer I was beside myself. I had lost my best friend. He was my guardian angel sent to me from above though, and continues to watch over me. I think of him often and say hello to him every time I walk into Mariucci Arena to go to work covering my beloved Gophers. The giant mural of

The Godfather...

him that covers the wall above the main foyer of the arena is so fitting, because he really was larger than life. I can see him from my radio booth up in the press box, staring over at me, and I know that he is looking down upon me proudly. It is like he is still taking care of me all these years later. What a wonderful man, I will never forget him.

Maroosh, as he was affectionately know, was such a colorful character. He spoke with that wonderful Iron Range accent, and was a real Minnesota treasure. He was so funny and was always telling jokes and pulling pranks, trying to make people laugh. And, despite the fact that he was known for being a legendary brawler, he was really just a teddy bear. He was actually an incredibly intelligent person. He was very knowledgeable about a wide range of topics and he loved history. He would read books constantly, even ones written in Russian. He was a real student of the game as well as a student of life. He hated to fly and would get drunker than hell before every flight. He was very proud of his ethnic heritage and loved to cook Italian food. And he was very giving to others, especially the less fortunate. He especially loved giving back to Camp Confidence, which meant so much to him.

John was always the center of attention, wherever he was, no matter what. People just gravitated towards him and wanted to be around him. There was just something about him. He made you feel safe and secure when you were around him. He was special, a real one-of-a-kind. The amazing thing about John was that as close as I felt to him, and considered him to be a father-figure and best friend, that there were probably a dozen other former players who felt exactly the same way about the guy. I know that Louie and Herbie felt that way about him too, which is just remarkable when you think about it. He truly is the godfather of Minnesota hockey. I really miss him.

You know, on a much lighter note, people always say that I am

The mural of big John always looking over me at Mariucci Arena...

such a good storyteller, which I take as a great compliment. But nobody told stories better than John. So, it is only fitting that I turn the tables on that tough old S.O.B. and share some of the classics that I have heard about him over the years. One of my favorites came from his wife, Gretchen, who was a lot younger than John and is really a beautiful lady. Well, one time they were in a restaurant together and John went up to the bar to order a drink. He apparently overheard a couple of drunk softball players talking to each other about him. One said to the other, "Hey, let's get rid of that old man and move in on his girl...". John heard them and yelled out "Who the hell called me an old man?" He then ran after the two guys and chased them out into the parking lot. As they were running out she heard one of the guys yell, "Oh my God, that's John Mariucci, we're going to die, HELP!" I guess he caught one of them and really let him have it. He then came back into the bar where the other guys in their group were gathered and said "I don't mind you making a play at my wife, but dammit don't ever call me an old man!"

The press loved him. He didn't care if he was politically correct or not, he just said whatever the hell was on his mind. If that offended someone, he didn't give a sh--. When he was coaching the Gophers he would occasionally hold his press conferences down in the locker room, where he would give interviews while doing chin ups buck-naked from the old steam-pipes. Could you imagine such a sight?

John was so tough. He loved to hit people and he loved to get hit. As a coach he encouraged his players to play tough and to never be intimidated or disrespected. He even told his players one time for an incentive that for every stitch they got, he would pay them $2 bucks. His fights with Blackjack Stewart when he was with the Blackhawks and Stewart was with Detroit, were legendary. They would go on for what seemed like an eternity. They would set ground rules for each other, like "the first

Here is my favorite painting by Terrence Fogarty of old Mariucci Arena

120

one to grab a jersey loses...", because in those days the refs would just let them go until they tied each other up. Then, afterward, they would go out and drink beer after the game and laugh about it. He was a real throwback. One of his former teammates with the Hawks, Bill Mosienko, recalled a game one time when an opposing player whacked his stick across John's back. He said that John just turned around, smiled, and then "beat the living hell out of him."

John Kundla, the former Gopher basketball coach told me a story one time when John was coaching the Gophers. He said that the Gophers had just lost to Michigan State and after the game John invited their coach, Amo Bessone, over for dinner. They were good buddies and gave each other hell all of the time. Apparently, John went to get Amo a drink, and then just before he handed it to him, he punched him right square in the nose and said "That's for beating us tonight!"

Another story I heard about John involved former Gopher football coach, Murray Warmath, who had apparently won some sort of national thumb-wrestling championship years ago. He would always taunt John to thumb-wrestle him, but John never would. Finally, after Murray egged him on in front of some of the players, John finally agreed to take him on. Sure enough, John wound up busting Murray's thumb.

I remember another story that one of the guys told me one time about how tough John was. He said that John was standing on the bench during a game one time, opening and closing the door when guys came on and off the ice. Well, he wasn't looking at one point and one of the guys slammed the door right on his hand. So, his hand is literally stuck in the door, crushed, and he very calmly says "Open the damn door...". I guess his hand was just a big swollen mess, but he didn't say a word. He acted like nothing had happened because he never wanted to admit he was hurt. He just kept a straight face and then started barking out orders to the guys on the ice as if nothing had happened.

Willard Ikola, who grew up in Eveleth with John, had a great story about a game that John was playing in one time late in his career with the Blackhawks against the team's minor league affiliate in Kansas City. I guess this young rookie who was trying to impress his coach cheap-shotted John by whacking him in the nose with his stick. John got pissed and skated after him. The kid, after realizing who he had just assaulted, jumped right over the boards and ran up the stairs through the stands. John jumped too and chased him right outside into the street. He was screaming at him the whole way as sparks flew from his

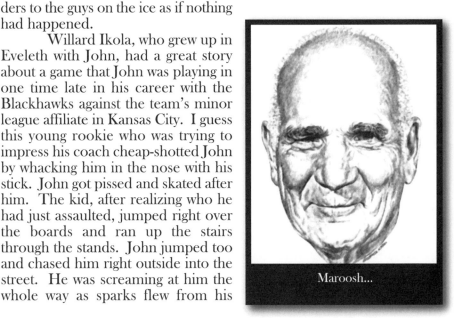

Maroosh...

skates as they scraped the concrete steps. Once he realized that he wasn't going to be able to catch him, he calmly walked back down the stairs on to the ice, even flirting with a few of the ladies in the crowd along the way. Apparently, he hopped back on to the ice and finished his shift like nothing had happened. Now, the teams played again the next night and John was still pretty upset because he had to get a bunch of stitches in that big nose of his. The organization wanted this kid to play though, because they were going to call him up and needed him to get some ice time. They also didn't want John to kill him either, so they went and talked to him to see if he would please leave the kid alone. John agreed, but only if the kid would come apologize to him. Sure enough, the kid came over to his hotel room all terrified and said he was sorry. John just smiled and told the kid to keep his damn stick down. I guess he even took the kid under his wing after that and showed him the ropes. That's the kind of guy John was, he would knock you down and then pick you back up again.

Wendy Anderson played for Maroosh back in the '50s and had another funny story. He said that back when he was running for governor a rival candidate was trying to discredit him by saying that he had no qualifications whatsoever, other than the fact that he was a great hockey player and that he had played for the Gophers. A reporter, wanting to follow up on the story, then interviewed John about what kind of a person Wendy was. John, seizing the opportunity, then made a big statement about how the allegations were totally false, saying: "Wendy was not a great hockey player, and the only reason he was even on my team was because I thought he might someday be governor..."

One of my former players, Gary Gambucci, had some great stories about John. One of my favorites happened in 1966, the year before I got there. The Gophers were playing on the road at Wisconsin, in what

Good times with Maroosh

was the first ever meeting between the two schools in the modern era. John had gone down a day early to speak to their booster club and told them that he was excited about the game and that it could potentially be a good rivalry down the road. He apparently said that once the Badgers get good enough to beat the Gophers, the rivalry would really take off. But, he didn't expect that to happen for at least five more years, figuring that they would need to get established with some coaches who could recruit, and what not.

Well, the next night the teams squared off and the Gophers were beating them in every imaginable way and even out-shot them something like 65-15. Wisconsin had this red hot goaltender from Roseau by the name of Gary Johnson though, and behind him they somehow beat the Gophers in overtime, 5-4. According to Gambooch, John was just madder than hell. In fact, he was so mad that he made them sit in the locker room after the game with their wet equipment on until everybody had left the arena. He told them that they had disgraced their mothers, their fathers, the University, themselves, and especially him. So, they just sat there, silent for the next hour or two, until the janitors eventually turned off all the lights in the arena. At that point John told them that they could finally take their damn skates off. John hated to lose, especially to teams like that, so I am sure he worked them like hell when they got back to Minneapolis too.

Gambooch tells another great story about his uncle, Elio Gambucci, who was a referee in the WCHA for years. He and John were having dinner one time up in North Dakota and someone had asked John how he had gotten such a big nose. People used to tease him about having the map of Italy carved out on his nose because it had been broken so many times. John then told the story about how one particular incident really busted it up for good. He said that it happened while he was playing for the Millers in a game one time against the Rochester Mustangs. He had apparently just gotten like a dozen stitches in the nose from a brawl he was in the night before and was looking to take it easy that particular game. Well, this kid by the name of Jack Bonner, a Mustangs defenseman who was an intern at the Mayo Clinic at the time, made the mistake of referring to John during the game as an "old man." John, of course, took offense to the remark and went after him. Bonner, in self defense, whacked John across the nose with his stick — splitting open the stitches he had just gotten from the night before. He was just a bloody mess I guess.

So, he goes down to the locker room to get fixed up, only he is so

Here's Maroosh trying to make peace between arch rivals Herbie and "Badger Bob" Johnson

123

upset that he says to hell with the stitches and just puts a big hunk of tape across his nose instead. He then raced back out there to get some payback. Sure enough, a little while later Bonner came skating across the red line and John just leveled him. He hit the kid so hard that it actually knocked him out cold and even ended his playing career. Well, according to Gambooch, the irony in the story came like 15 years later when John was called to his dying mother's bedside up in Eveleth. Once there, she is telling him that she is feeling well and to not worry about her because her doctor was taking such good care of her. She went on and on, describing him as a sweet, gentle, comforting man who she just adored. John was so grateful for this guy and everything he had done for his poor mother that he wanted to meet him and thank him. Just then the guy walked in and his mom proudly introduced him to Dr. Bonner. I guess he and John hit it off immediately and just laughed like hell. He couldn't wait to show him how his nose had healed up and taken on the shape of Italy.

There is one last great story about John that I had heard years ago about his time in the Service. During the war, John served in the Coast Guard and was stationed in Staten Island, just outside of New York City. While there, he played for the Coast Guard Cutters, a legendary team of NHL players who were all stationed at the same military base together. Now, unlike most young men during World War II, John never had to go overseas. He did, however, take the Staten Island ferry to get to the mainland to play hockey at night. In the meantime, Sam LoPresti, a former teammate of his with the Blackhawks who was also from Eveleth, had been sent off to serve overseas in the Navy. Sure enough, the merchant ship that he was on got torpedoed and sunk by a German submarine. Sam then wound up shipwrecked alone in a lifeboat, floating off the coast of South America until finally being rescued after 42 nights at sea. Well, the irony came after the war had ended, when John got this big maritime medal by the Coast Guard for his courageous service and bravery for going overseas, which in this case was the Hudson River. Poor Sam, meanwhile, who nearly died of thirst and sharks, got absolutely nothing. John used to tease him about it all the time and just drive him nuts by carrying around that medal.

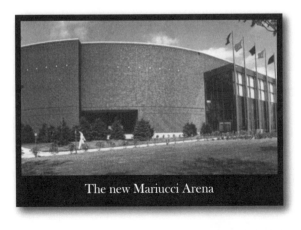

The new Mariucci Arena

124

Ch. 13
A Toast to the Future

As I sit back and think about all of the events that have unfolded over the years I can't help but get nostalgic. Losing my eye was maybe even a mixed blessing as I look back on it now. While it was a terrible and tragic thing to have happen, it got me together with John and ultimately set me on my career path into coaching. I will never know, but I have no regrets on how it all worked out. Being a teacher and coach made for a wonderful career. I wasn't the best X's and O's coach with regards to systems and strategy, but I had a love for the game. I think that came through in my style. I really wanted my guys to play with a passion and play like hell. If we had to mix it up out there then that is what we had to do sometimes. Hockey is a tough game and I loved every bit of it.

Even though my style varied a lot at the various levels that I coached at, some things remained the same. I mean I coached in high school, juniors, college, the minors and in the pros, but I learned early on that as long as you treated your players with respect, were honest with them and cared about them, then you would be successful. My whole life was sports and I was just so lucky to have the opportunity to live out my dreams. Coaching kids was a wonderful experience and to see them succeed was just great. Sure, I loved the competition and I loved winning, but I also got great satisfaction from seeing my players do their best and then go on to have happy and productive lives after hockey.

As for the secret to my success, if there is such a thing, I guess it would be that I had a real passion for the game of hockey. I also cared about my players very, very much. My players knew that I would be straight forward and honest with them and that they could believe what I was telling them. Sure, I made mistakes, but they were honest mistakes and I think my players knew that. So, I worked hard and did the best I could so that my team would come out on top. I also believed in sticking to things and following through with them. I just believed that you had to take whatever God given talent you had and then use it to the best of your ability. I would also add that having a great sense of humor really helps too. Everybody can use a good laugh every now and then, and that is what really keeps you young at heart.

To all the fans who supported me over the years, all I can say is thank you. The hockey fans here are absolutely wonderful. They supported me through thick and thin and I really appreciated that so much. From the Gophers to the Saints to the North Stars, to the Moose, they were just amazing. Fans still stop me on the street to talk to me and that just means the world to me. It is so wonderful to have people come up to me and tell me that they enjoyed watching my games when I was coaching, or that they enjoy listening to me now on the radio for Gopher games.

As for my legacy, I just hope to be remembered as a good person. I suppose that when it is all said and done, I would hope to be thought of as somebody who cared a great deal about his players; as somebody who cared very much about winning; as somebody who did the best job he could to help his team win; as somebody who just enjoyed every minute of what he was doing; and as somebody who was very appreciative that he had the chance to do what he loved to do for a living for as long as he did. I would also hope to be remembered as a good father and grandfather. That would mean a lot too.

As a coach, it means so much to me to hear from former players who tell me that they enjoyed playing for me and that they learned something along the way. I want all of my former players to know that I really cared about them too, and not just as players but as people. I tried to treat them with respect and was honest with them. Beyond that, I always tried to do my best both on and off the ice. I just always felt blessed to be able to make my living doing what I loved doing. I have never had a real job in my life, it has always been in the world of hockey. What a lucky guy I am to be able to say that at this stage of life.

It was such a privilege to be involved with so many great teams and so many great people along the way. I just can't thank them enough for the love and support that they gave me over the years. I endured plenty of screw-ups and set-backs, that is for sure, but I would like to think that I learned from them and was able to grow as a person. Sure, I have suffered some adversities in my life, but I never felt sorry for myself. I knew that there were always people much worse off than me. Yeah, I lost an eye that cost me my hockey career, but at least I could still see. I just always tried to count my blessings and stay positive in life.

I am also so happy to be able to help others who also suffer from alcoholism. That might be my biggest accomplishment in life, more than anything else. I feel that things happen for a reason in our lives and as such I am committed to helping those who can't seem to beat this terrible disease. I wouldn't be able to help them had I not gone through it myself though, and seen first hand just how destructive it can be. There is a saying in our fellowship that says "We will not regret the past, nor wish to shut the door on it." I believe strongly in that and use those life experiences, both good and bad, to help guide others on their way to sobriety.

Sure, as I reflect back upon my life I do have some regrets from along the way. Mostly, I am so sorry to those whose lives became adversely effected from my long and difficult battle with alcohol. My problems with the disease have been many, and I know that I hurt a lot of people in my day. I do feel shame and sadness for that, yet I have forgiven myself and can only now look positively towards the future. I am just so happy that I was finally able to beat it. I also regret the fact that I didn't get to know my father as the person I had always imagined him to be. He suffered from alcoholism his entire adult life and was never able to beat it. I am sad for him that he never got shown the way out, because I am sure deep down he was a good man. I am also sorry about not being able to spend more quality time with my mother. We lost her in 1999 at the age of 95. What a lady she was. She always took care of me and was truly the glue that held our family together when times were tough. I loved her so deeply and miss her very much. The only other regret that I have in life is that I never got to play hockey for the Gophers. Thank God that I was able to at least get my degree there, which means the world to me.

All in all, I have had a wonderful, rich, fulfilling life. I have a fantastic daughter and two amazing grandkids, who I love very much. I also have a wonderful sister, who has a great husband and two boys who are all great Toronoto Maple Leafs fans. I am blessed to be here today and don't take anything for granted in this life. I'm just grateful for all I've been given. This honor, a life in hockey, it's wonderful. I should be retired and living in Florida, but here I am having the time of my life. I hope it lasts forever.

Lastly, I think it is important to say thanks to those who have helped me to overcome my addiction to alcohol over the years. Without them, I honestly don't know if I would be here today. I will be indebted to them forever. The only way I can repay them is to pay it forward and try to help others. Fortunately, I was able to beat this terrible disease. It is not over though, because I struggle with it every single day of my life. I am so proud to say, however, that as of January 18th, 2008, I have been sober for exactly 25 years. Over that time my life has certainly changed a great deal. In fact, it would seem that I have had two separate groups of friends over the past quarter century of sobriety — my hockey friends and my friends of Bill W. For those of you who don't know, Bill W. was the founder of the wonderful 12-step fellowship program that saved my life.

Normal people can't understand the absolute control this disease

My sweet mother, my hero...

127

can have on a person. And believe me, it is a hideous disease. What I like to say to people who are alcoholics or to those who have alcoholics in their lives is that we're not bad people trying to get good, we're sick people trying to get well. The wonderful thing about it all though is that there is a solution that works for everybody who will commit to it and do it. That is what our fellowship is all about. I can't refer to it by name, but for those millions of people who know about and are a part of it, they swear by it.

I am so grateful to all of the men and women who have been there for me and helped me to not only get clean, but to stay clean. Believe it or not, even after all this time the most important thing in my life is that I don't take a drink. That is where it starts and stops for me, every single day of my life. It is not a religious program, but rather a spiritual one. There is a big difference. We don't want it to be about religion. For some, that is what drives them, but for others it is something completely different. It is just about surrendering to a higher power, whether that is a god or a support group doesn't matter. We just want the people who want to get help, to be able to get help.

I went to my first meeting in 1970, shortly after getting arrested for drunk driving. That was a tough time for me. The news got in the paper and it was very embarrassing for me and my family. I didn't get sober, however, until 1983, some 13 years later. So, sometimes it takes time for it all to sink in. I eventually surrendered to the disease though, and that was when I finally got the help I so desperately needed. From that moment on, I have constantly surrounded myself with people who understand where I have been and where I want to get to. I try to go to meetings every single day, and when I can't, I think about being there and about what I need to do to stay sober. It is unequivocally the most important thing in my life.

Norvy Mulligan was a great guy and one of the first people who helped me in my recovery as a sponsor. He saw my name in the paper following that DWI 37 years ago and got a hold of me to see if I needed some help. I met him and I tried to get my problem in order, but I wasn't ready to surrender yet. I didn't really think I had a problem at that point and was in denial. I don't know when the transition was exactly when I went from being a problem drinker to a full-fledged alcoholic. But it happened.

One of the characteristics of an alcoholic is that he or she denies it, then he or she minimalizes it, and then he or she thinks they can control it. I went through all of those stages before I finally got help. I believe all alcoholics have a moment of truth in their life when they finally cry out for help and accept that the disease is killing them. We call that the "point of pitiful and incomprehensible demoralization." For me, it came in a dark motel room up in Toronto back in 1983. We have to admit that we can't beat it by ourselves, because if we could have, we would have done so long ago. As we say in our fellowship, we ask for help from a god of our understanding. It says in our big book that if we don't keep ourselves in a fit spiritual condition, then the time will come when we will drink again and we won't know why. We are alcoholics, the normal thing for us to do is drink. It is our obsession. So, we need to stay sober one day at a time. That is the bottom line.

Sadly, alcoholism runs in my family. My grandfather was an alcoholic; my father was an alcoholic; I am an alcoholic and my daughter is an alcoholic. It is not a genetic disease, but if there is a history in your family then you are certainly at a higher risk. If you grow up in that lifestyle then I believe that you are more susceptible to falling under its spell.

As for me, I wasn't an everyday drinker. I was what they call a spree-drinker. I wanted to have fun and kick up my heels and then go home. I was also a good liar and got away with a lot. I was good at hiding my condition. I thought I had it under control. I thought I understood it. I thought that the knowledge I had obtained from some of the best treatment facilities in the world would save me. I thought I had will power. I vigorously defended my right to drink. I was wrong.

One of the things we learn in our fellowship is that alcoholics tend to seek out lower companions after a while. You know, I wasn't the kind of person who had a bottle hidden in the drawer, rather I was the type of person who went out to bars to drink beer. But, because I was a recognizable public figure when I was coaching, I tended to go to some pretty off-the-beaten-path kind of bars so that nobody would recognize me. It wasn't a very pleasant experience, going to those types of seedy bars, but those are the lengths we will go to in order to satisfy ourselves. It didn't matter where I was because when I started to drink I thought I was rich and invisible. I would be buying drinks for everybody and figured that nobody would know who I was. It was crazy, it really was.

Another saying in our fellowship that says it is not the third or seventh or ninth drink that gets you, it is the first one. Even right now, at

Here I am with my two wonderful grandkids, Christopher & Michael

this very moment, if I went out and started drinking again, I would be in deep, deep trouble very quickly. I see people come back to our meetings all the time who have tried and failed. I have been there, believe me. You know, we have another saying that says people who don't go to meetings, don't get to find out what happens to people who don't go to meetings. When people stop going to meetings, they get complacent and eventually they fall of the wagon.

When I finally did get sober, it was tough to go back to work. Being in sports, alcohol is such a part of the fabric of our lives. It is everywhere. That is the sporting culture. Whether it is a victory bottle of champagne or a beer after practice with the guys out on the road, it just becomes like second nature after a while. It was so engrained into every facet of my life that I just didn't think I could ever get away from it. I was absolutely terrified. At first, I just wanted to run and get away from it all. You learn to adapt though, and that is the same for everybody in recovery. Life isn't over, it just changes — and trust me, it is for the better.

There were times over the years when it was tough to go out with people after I was sober and to see them drinking. People who didn't know my situation would oftentimes say "Glen, can I buy you a drink?" I would usually just politely say no thanks, but on occasion I would try to make light of the situation by saying "Hell yes, you can buy me a thousand drinks!" Humor is always the best policy in those types of situations I have always found. One time in a bar a waitress asked me if I wanted a drink, to which I replied "No thanks, I am allergic to alcohol." She then said "Really, that is unusual." I said "If I drink it I break out in spots." "Spots?" she said curiously. "Yeah... New York, Boston, Chicago...".

Then, if people ever bought me a bottle of wine or liquor for some reason, I would just say thank you and then give it away. I am sure that every person who has struggled with this disease or is in recovery can

My dear mother and my sister, Jean

relate to what I am talking about. For the most part, people have always been extremely understanding of my situation and usually try to make me feel comfortable. It doesn't bother me if people drink around me anymore, I have gotten way past that in my recovery. Nobody is going to force you to drink if you don't want to, and I always remember that. Holidays and times like that were tough for me early on, but I got through it. It was tough, but I wouldn't go back down that road for all the money in the world.

When we drink we are so full of shame and guilt for what we have done. We have all hurt others along the way. All of us. My first marriage ended in a disaster and most of the blame can fall squarely on my shoulders due to my addiction to alcohol. It had a lot to do with the failure of my second marriage too. It also got between my daughter and I, when I wasn't there for her like I should have been. For us, whenever we allow that poison into our systems, it immediately takes away our ability to make intelligent decisions. It is so hard to understand if you are not one. But that is what happens to alcoholics.

My fellowship has prepared me for the future though. I know that if I have a hardship in my family or if something, God forbid, terrible happens, that I will be OK. I know that I can lean on them in the hard times, just in case. Things will come up in life, like health issues and what not, so we have to have a plan. It is so comforting to know that I have the tools to deal with those situations should they present themselves. That gives me so much peace of mind.

My mother was my hero, she really was. I got sober when she was 79 years old and she lived to be nearly 96. So, the greatest joy of my life came from me knowing that for the last 17 years that she walked this earth she had a sober son. It was so nice to be able to spend time with her while I was sober and to get to know her all over again. She was the one person in our family who provided stability for me. My dad was an alcoholic and was always in and out of our lives. My mother was a pillar in my life and I am so grateful for that. You know, I was always such a well intentioned young man. The problem was that people judge you by your actions rather than your intentions. I always wanted to do this or do that for my mother, but somehow, someway, alcohol always found a way to get in between that and prevented me from doing the right things. When you are in the throws of alcoholism, there is always something that seems like it is more fun or more important to do. I am glad I was able to atone for that later in life.

My big brother Jake

So much of what we did to hurt people that loved us were errors of omission, rather than commission. When I was in the height of my alcoholism I was unable to be there for those who needed me most, particularly my mom and my daughter. One of the toughest struggles I ever had in life was being able to forgive myself for some of those things. I will never forget when my sponsor made me hold up a mirror to my face, at which point he gave me the verdict: "Not Guilty." I had been sober for some time when that happened but I had been struggling with all of the guilt for a long time. He said it was OK to get rid of the shame of what happened in the past. He assured me that it was time for me to forgive myself and move on. He explained to me the difference between shame and guilt. Guilt is OK. Guilt is about making mistakes, which you can do something about it to correct. Shame, however, is when you tell yourself that you ARE a mistake and there is nothing you can do about it. So, I stopped being a victim and I accepted responsibility for my actions.

I remember when I got arrested for drunk driving back in 1970. My daughter was a sophomore at Richfield High School at the time. I was running around trying to save my job at the time, doing damage control. I was in self-preservation mode and in so doing, I completely ignored her feelings. I am sure the kids in school made some comments about it because it was in the news and I am sure she felt just terrible. Years later I asked her about that and she felt awful about the fact that I never talked to her about it. So, I felt just sick about that. I was not the best father when I was drinking and I am very sorry about that. Sadly, she too became an alcoholic. Fortunately, she has been sober for six years now and I am so proud of her. Luckily, when she was getting sober I was able to be there for her and was able to be a better father. I was 18 years sober by then and was able to talk to her. She lives in Phoenix and is fine now. She is a great mother and has really turned her life around. I am so lucky to have her in my life, she means everything to me.

My wonderful daughter, Kate

For me, my purpose in life now is to help others. And, if I can use my celebrity or notoriety through hockey as a means to speak to people, then so be it. I enjoy talking to groups and if hockey is an ice breaker, then that is just fine. I was able to overcome my own demons and now to be able to help others do the same is beyond rewarding. To watch others who have battled the disease like I did to get better is amazing. It is such a joy to see. The reward is the irrefutable evidence as to how much better people's lives are once they stop drinking. You get to see them rediscover how great life can be all over again.

I go to the Thunderbird Hotel every morning at 7:30 and order two poached eggs, three strips of bacon and a cup of coffee. I have my own booth and my favorite waitress, Jody, takes good care of me. She comes over and just says, "Good morning Glen, will it be the usual?" Then I make myself available to talk to other people from my fellowship. The secret of sobriety is for one alcoholic to talk to another. We talk to each other and see how we are doing. We support each other. I have gotten calls at three in the morning from people who I have to talk down off the proverbial ledge. I have seen it all over these past 25 years, the good, the bad and the ugly. That is all part of the deal. When you sign up to help people and put yourself out there, then those things are going to happen from time to time.

I just think about all of the sponsors that I had early on and about all of the people who I called up to talk to over the years. The reason our fellowship works so well is because those who have surrendered and gone into recovery work tirelessly to help those who are still trying to get to that point. We all help each other in this group and that is what it is all about. Just like realtors say "location-location-location," we say "meetings-meetings-meetings." You have to come to the meetings and you have to get tied into a support group that will not only be there for you, but also hold you accountable for your actions. It is the key to every one of our members' success. To go from one side of the table to the other though, that is pretty sweet. When you can go from being helped to helping others, wow, what a wonderful feeling. In fact, I would say that it is every bit as good as scoring a game-winning goal in front of a packed house at Madison Square Garden.

I just hope that in some small way this book might help some people who are going through what I went through to get help. I also hope that it will encourage others who have gotten through it to give back to those who are less fortunate or who can't seem to help themselves. That is what this is all about. As I said before, this wonderful fellowship teaches us to live a sober life one day at a time. For me, as of January 18th, 2008, I am proud to say that I have religiously done just that for exactly 9,125 days in a row. And do you know what? They have been the best 25 years of my life, without question. Nothing comes close to tell you the truth. So, as I look to the future I am both grateful and optimistic. I can't wait for the 50th anniversary. Hopefully there will be plenty of Gopher National Championships and Wild Stanley Cups to celebrate along the way.

Here's to the next 25 years!

Thank you all from the bottom of my heart...

133

Dear Dad,

I have always been proud to be your daughter. I have always been proud of you. But perhaps most importantly, at different times and for different reasons, it has always been wonderful to be your daughter.

When I was younger, I was the "coach's daughter". Which meant my friends and I went to hockey games; cheering for the beloved Gophers, getting crazy with the Fighting Saints and living and dying with the North Stars. Through it all, it was wild and it was fun. After all, it was hockey!

Sports occupy a different world, hockey an even more select island. Hockey players talk differently, think differently and look at life differently. I have found a life in hockey is an unusual life; a long life in hockey an extremely unusual life. But that is what you have done and done with such passion and integrity. You may be making your notes on hockey programs while the world is on laptop, but there isn't much about hockey you don't know.

Yet, as much as hockey is a large part of your life, you live in a world more broadly defined. You may have won a lot of hockey games but it is the other victories that are more glorious in your life. And I have been proud to be a part of that.

I hope I inherited your sense of humor. I know I inherited your walk. You did teach me all those great locker-room maxims and to "play with the minor hurts". I wouldn't change a thing and I never want to forget a story. There are some truly amazing stories.

Well, Dad — "Luck is the residue of design". We've been lucky Dad, but we worked hard. I love you and always will.

Love,

Kate

I thought it would be fitting for Glen's daughter, Kate, to have the last word...

ABOUT THE AUTHOR

Born and raised in Fairmont, Minn., best-selling sports author Ross Bernstein grew up loving sports and went on to attend the University of Minnesota. It was there where he first got into writing through some rather unique circumstances. You see, after a failed attempt to make it as a walk-on to the University's top-ranked Golden Gopher hockey team, Ross opted for the next best thing — to become the team's mascot, *"Goldy the Gopher."* His humorous accounts as a mischievous rodent then inspired the 1992 regional best-seller: *"Gopher Hockey by the Hockey Gopher."* The rest, they say... is history!

After spending the next five years in Chicago and New York working as vice president of marketing for a start-up children's entertainment company, Ross decided to take a leap of faith and come home to pursue his dream of becoming a full-time sports author. Since then, he has written nearly 40 books, ranging from critically acclaimed national biographies, to regional best-selling coffee-table sports history books, to inspirational children's memoirs. As a result, he has been featured as a guest on more than 1,000 local and national television and radio programs over his career, including: *CNN* and *ESPN*, among others, and was even featured on the covers of the *Wall Street Journal* and *USA Today.*

As a sought after motivational speaker, Ross speaks to corporations and groups around the country about the inspirational legacy of the late hall of fame hockey coach Herb Brooks. Ross, who had actually been working with Brooks on writing a series of motivational/self-help books at the time of his tragic passing in the Summer of 2003, decided to honor his friend and mentor by turning their project into a living memorial. The result was the nationally critically acclaimed biography entitled *"Remembering Herbie."* Ross further honored Brooks in 2006 when he wrote the motivational-biography entitled *"America's Coach: Life Lessons & Wisdom for Gold Medal Success."*

Ross Bernstein

To keep his legacy alive, Ross speaks about the influence Brooks had on the world of sports, his unorthodox leadership style, and about the impact of the now legendary 1980 U.S. Olympic hockey *"Miracle on Ice,"* which will forever live on as one of the greatest moments in the history of sports. Putting many of the life-lessons and ideologies he learned from the fiery coach into a practical business application, his presentation aims to inspire others to follow their dreams and maybe, just maybe, even create their own miracles.

Ross and his wife Sara have a five year-old daughter and presently reside in Eagan, Minn.